ON ▪ THE ▪ ROUNDS ▪ W

MEDICS

ON · THE · ROUNDS · WITH
MEDICS

PETER HAINING

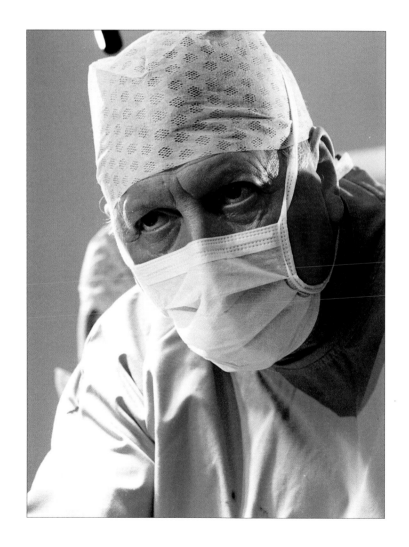

B⬚XTREE

G R A N A D A   T E L E V I S I O N

First published in Great Britain in 1995 by Boxtree Limited

Text © Granada Television Ltd 1995
Photographs © Granada Television Ltd 1995

10 9 8 7 6 5 4 3 2 1

Designed by Anita Ruddell

Printed and bound in Great Britain by Cambus Litho, East Kilbride, Glasgow for

Boxtree Limited
Broadwall House
21 Broadwall
London   SE1 9PL

A CIP catalogue entry for this book is available from the British Library.

ISBN 0 7522 1006 8

CONTENTS

Acknowledgements

My special thanks are due to the following for their help in the writing of this book: Louise Berridge, Terry Reeve, John Friend Newman, Claire McCourt, Lynnette Carroll, Linda Strath, all of the members of the cast and crew who made my days with them such an enjoyable experience and, particularly, Sue Johnston and Tom Baker, for their kindness and good nature.

THE SHOW THE REAL
MEDICS
WATCH

'MEDICS', the continuing story of Henry Park Trust Hospital is unique among television medical drama series. It is now filmed very largely in a former Manchester hospital that has been specially refurbished for the programme. Launched originally as the story of a group of medical students training to be doctors, it has now been transformed into a full-blown serial about all aspects of hospital life. It has also provided image-changing roles for two familiar faces who were previously associated with legendary TV programmes: Tom Baker of 'Doctor Who' and Sue Johnston of 'Brookside'. And unlike a lot of other series, it is filmed rather than taped on video, which gives it an added sense of realism.

The series is also a tribute to the determination of Sally Head, the drama chief at Granada, to build an audience; as well as to the six producers who, with a company of talented actors and a hard-working production team have created a show which despite its ups and downs is now in its fifth year. TV Quick wrote of 'Medics' in September 1994, 'This is the show that real medics watch without creasing up with incredulity.'

Several other reviewers have been equally enthusiastic about it: Adam Sweeting writing a month earlier in the *Guardian* said, 'This is enthralling stuff, cramming together fifty-seven varieties of human relationships with strong ethical-political issues coloured bright red so you can't miss them . . . nervous viewers may need a course of tranquillizers.' Adding weight to this verdict was Maureen Paton of the *Daily Express* who wrote that same month: ' "Medics" is no cynical "Cardiac Arrest" exercise, out to undermine the medical profession. Its (transplanted) heart is always in the right place.' And Simon London of the *Daily Mirror* also concurred, 'Although the problems facing the NHS are highlighted in the series, "Medics" is in many ways the acceptable face of hospital drama.'

None of the critics, however, have

Left: The two stars who have contributed so much towards the success of 'Medics', Sue Johnston (Ruth Parry) and Tom Baker (Professor Geoffrey Hoyt).

Above: The group of actors who launched the original 'Medics' in 1990, photographed in front of 'Henry Park Hospital' - Hope Hospital, Salford.

been in any doubt about the importance of the contributions of the two major stars. The usually ascerbic *Time Out* declaring, 'Tom Baker's performance is too big for the screen by rights, but it works brilliantly – you can't take your eyes off him.' While the *Daily Express*'s always outspoken Margaret Forwood wrote, 'Sue Johnston is compelling as the hard-nosed Ruth Parry – a woman who's not afraid to make enemies of the doctors or the patients.'

All this praise is a long way from the original series in 1990, which earned the epithet 'Bed-ics' for the number of times its characters hopped into bed with each other. Just as the series' new home in the refurbished Ancoats Hospital on the outskirts of Manchester is a world apart from some of the locations the production team had to utilize in earlier series –

including a disused mental institution at Prestwich, which with its padded cells and lack of running water or heat was 'always creepy and often frightening,' according to one of the long-serving crew members. (Today the site is about to be occupied by a new Tesco supermarket.)

Whatever the conditions in which they worked, the backroom team of 'Medics' always strove to give the series a sense of authenticity, and as many as five different working hospitals have been used over the years for scenes in general wards, intensive care units and operating theatres – all while the rest of the premises were busy with real patients. Such experiences have combined to give members of the team a sense of 'family' which is still evident as they work today. Indeed, the success of 'Medics' owes as much to those behind the cameras as to those who appeared in front of it. 'We've all become a bit of an institution,' as one of the crew light-heartedly puts it.

Certainly this is a message that the present producer, Louise Berridge, echoes on behalf of those who occupied her chair before: Julia Smith, Esta Charkham, Gub Neil, Tony Dennis and Alison Lumb. It is their stories – and those of the cast who have starred in 'Medics' – which are told in the pages of this book.

Louise Berridge is an exuberant figure with curly, fair hair whose youthful looks belie her considerable experience in television. Now a freelance producer, she worked for a number of years in pop-

Professor Geoffrey Hoyt (Tom Baker), Henry Park's 'benevolent tyrant'.

ular drama – including a happy stint on 'Boon' for Central TV – and also on several drama documentaries which she believes gave her invaluable experience in the techniques of research.

In 1993 fate took her on to the production team of the BBC's 'EastEnders', also the brainchild of 'Medics' creator Julia Smith. (See page 16).

'While I was in charge of the storylines, the show's audience went up from 17 million to 25 million,' she says. 'It is the thing I am most proud of to date, and in fact my material will still be going through until this August just before 'Medics' is back on the screen!'

Louise joined 'Medics' as script editor for the fourth series, and then when ill-health meant that the producer Alison Lumb was unable to continue in charge for the fifth series, Louise was invited by Granada to fill the vacant chair – just two weeks before shooting was due to start.

'It's been pretty hectic ever since then,' she says. 'There was obviously a lot of work to do and the storylines were in a state of change. The series has been hovering around the 9 million viewer mark and I'm determined to push this up to 12 million.'

Louise has been watching 'Medics' since series three, and believes that a lot of people have either forgotten or didn't watch the first two. She herself has no medical connections in her family,

although she did spend some time in hospital as a child.

'This is my first contact with a medical series and I live by a little book called the *Oxford Handbook of Clinical Medicine*,' she says. 'It is the one that all the house officers carry around with them. I actually found it rather depressing. Because under such headings as "How to fit an endotracheal tube" it says things like, "Ask the nurse to try one more time and by watching her you might get an idea of how to do it." It can easily cause all your illusions about hospitals and doctors to crumble very quickly!'

In fact, as Louise is quick to point out, 'Medics' has a highly qualified group of experts to call upon to make sure that everything shown or discussed on the screen is correct.

'We have three medical advisers who work in rotation with the scriptwriters right from the moment they are commissioned to create an episode for the series,' she explains. 'They will give advice, vet scripts and even make some valuable suggestions. It's wonderful to have someone on tap to whom you can say, "Can you give me a good disease for this patient?" '

The three script consultants are Dr Gareth Williams of St James's Hospital, Leeds; Dr Andrew Millar of the Royal London Hospital and Dr John Williams of St Mary's Paddington. There is also a nursing adviser, John Wickens of the London Nurses Agency. The equally crucial element of showing as realistically as possible the many different illnesses and injuries handled by the hospital is the work of make-up supervisors Linda Strath and Margaret O'Keefe. They need constant access to the on-set nursing adviser, Dympna Donegan (*see 'The Blood and Gore Team'*).

In most discussions in the press and the media about 'Medics', comparisons are invariably drawn between the series and its great rival on BBC, 'Casualty'. Sometimes even the other more recent additions to the genre including 'Cardiac Arrest', 'ER' and 'Chicago Hope' are compared. Louise Berridge wastes no time in spelling out the essential differences in the Granada production.

'"Casualty" may always get bigger ratings than "Medics",' she says with disarming candour, 'because it is simpler, easier to understand and the political elements are put in a very black and white way. You don't have to think too deeply – just sit back and enjoy it. We are just not of the same school – I think we should be aiming at the same audiences that watch "Prime Suspect" or "Cracker" or "Band of Gold". Sally Head is as much behind "Medics" as she is the force behind these others. I don't want people to say that here is another medical drama like "Casualty" – instead, here is a serious adult drama.

'"Medics" also has one huge advantage over most of the rest which I want to exploit. That is the fact that it is transmitted at 9pm which means we are post-watershed and we are able to do things that the others are not. I don't just mean in terms of gore and having lots of bonking scenes – but putting things on an adult level.

'I believe another of its strengths is the serial element which is stronger than in any other medical series. Viewers do become engaged by individual characters and like to follow them through. These are always the stories that work best for us. We are also fortunate in having two good names in Tom Baker and Sue Johnston.'

Louise pauses as if searching her mind for further amunition to augment her case. 'It is also a fact that we can be more adult than "Casualty", she says. 'We can really explore controversial stories on topics like AIDS or lesbianism and we know that audiences really appreciate that. In fact we did some audience research before beginning work on the fifth series and that was the verdict that came back to us time and time again.'

'I know some people argue that there are elements of "Medics" that are the same as you would find in a soap. But I don't agree with that. Viewers understand a lot more than they are often given credit for, and we never patronize our audience as I believe some

Dr Robert Nevin (James Gaddas), Henry Park's handsome heart-breaker in an intimate moment during the second series with Abbi Roux.

of the other medical dramas do. We put our audience through the ringer instead!'

Among Louise's plans for the fifth series are a new title sequence – 'the old one was very similar to "Casualty" even to the colour scheme,' she says – and storylines to make it more controversial.

'I think we have to deal with some subjects that television normally avoids,' she continues. 'The political wrangling has always been there and is an important element of the series. But the big problem we have is that you cannot make a series honestly about hospitals or doctors without tackling some of the serious issues of under-funding and basic abuse of the system. However, we do not want 'Medics' to be a party political broadcast. What we can do is introduce

Hospital Administrator Ruth Parry (Sue Johnston) under attack for her policies at a press conference in the fourth series.

characters who will bring in opposing viewpoints and in so doing become the characters the viewers love or hate according to their own inclinations.'

Louise is also keen on the use of comedy and admires the strong elements of black comedy to be heard in the American series 'ER' – though she believes "Medics" offers more humour than any of its rival British medical dramas.

'But what I most like about working on "Medics" is the opportunity it gives you to deal with people at moments of severe emotional crisis,' she goes on. 'It is not just the medical technicalities that are interesting – it is the people, and I hope that will show even more strongly in the fifth series. And where we are going for an issue that affects people we are really going for it.

'My fear has always been that if you introduce topics to be controversial you must do them for real or you can so easily trivialize them. Take homosexual storylines as an example. There is always the risk of being accused of bringing them in for the sake of an issue and that invariably weakens the drama. We have a situation like this between two doctors, Sarah Kemp and Liz Seymour, in the next series – but it's a love story. It is not about, "Guess what, she's gay!". For the minute you do that you demean the whole story and you certainly demean your own characters.'

Another of the problems that Louise invariably faces – and one which is rarely evident to viewers – is the limitations of where the various doctors can work and their specialities.

'There is always a danger if you concentrate on the general ward, for instance, that you end up with endless stories about bowels and abscesses. It's very easy to bore your audience. So I'm planning to move some of the doctors around and make full use of all the facilities we've got in Ancoats. I'm also planning to introduce a new female character in paediatrics because it is one of those areas where you can mix some of the other specialisms. And I'm planning to kill someone off – but just who will certainly have to remain a secret for the time being!

'Above all else,' Louise says by way of summing up her policy for 'Medics', 'we have to tell a good story – for without that there is nothing. You can certainly introduce all the medical elements you like, but you still need a good story. There is this awful assumption in some quarters that by putting in stories that people want to watch you are somehow cheapening a series. I just don't see why you can't make popular drama that is *good!* '

For someone who has been pitched into the producer's chair at such short notice, Louise Berridge has very clear ideas about the direction that the series will take and makes no bones about her determination to increase the size of the audience dramatically.

And few would probably disagree that it is no more than 'Medics' deserves after five years of endeavour that have seen it transformed from a modest six-part summer fill-in programme to a twelve-episode, prime-time autumn series . . .

THE TRANSFUSION OF MEDICS

THE ORIGINAL CONCEPT for 'Medics' came from the astute mind of TV producer, Julia Smith – although her idea was somewhat different from the series which is seen today. It was also an idea, to quote a long-serving member of the production team, that 'had three producers before a single episode was seen on television'.

Julia, whose name is as familiar to the general public as it is within television circles – especially for her most famous creation, the BBC's long-running soap, 'EastEnders' – first discussed her idea for a new series with Granada's innovative drama supremo, Sally Head, in 1989. But what she had in mind was not another medical soap: rather a series for the next decade which focused on the lives of a group of medical students in a training hospital.

Television series and dramas about hospital life have, of course, been a familiar feature on the small screen for years. From ATV's pioneer twice-weekly serial, 'Emergency – Ward Ten' which ran from 1957 to 1967 and made a star of Australian actor Charles Tingwell, who played a house doctor; by way of the BBC's story of a rural Scottish practise,

'Dr Finlay's Casebook', which notched up over 150 episodes between 1959-1966; and 'Doctor in the House', London Weekend's ninety-episode comedy series in 1970-1973 – to name just three of the earlier classics – medical dramas have now exerted a unique fascination on viewers for almost half a century. 'Medics', however, was planned as something rather different: a series which was not solely hospital-based, but looked at the intricacies and intimacies of the lives of four final-year students; their tutor, a sympathetic female registrar; and a hard-pressed houseman.

'Sexy, compelling, incisive and fun,' are the adjectives that the versatile producer Gub Neal uses to describe the 'Medics' which he finally brought to the screen in the summer of 1990. 'It was never going to be another show about life in a hospital. What we wanted to do was to lift the lid on what really happens to some medical students in their last year of study as they face the challenges of success and failure in a difficult and sometimes dangerous profession. It was going to be a kind of "Twentysomething" for the Nineties,' Gub adds, drawing a parallel to Edward Zwick's

One of the earliest stunts seen on 'Medics' was this abseiling sequence, filmed for the first series on top of a Manchester tower block. A mixture of actors and stuntmen performed the tricky manoeuvre which appeared as an event during Henry Park's student rag week. Amongst the extras who appeared in the sequence was Jimmi Harkishin, who would later return to the series as House Officer Dr Jay Rahman.

spectacularly successful TV series 'thirtysomething' about a bunch of middle-class friends caught in the half-light between maturity and middle age.

The plan was for six, hour-long episodes focusing on four students: Jessica Hardman (played by Penny Bunton), Annie Chung (Su Lin-Looi), Niall McGuiness (Robert Patterson), Alex Taylor (Peter Wingfield), and also the Registrar Dr Claire Armstrong (Francesca Ryan) and houseman Iraj Iravani (Eric Loren). Each story would explore their aspirations and dreams, their fears and anxieties: all seen in the context of a high-powered hospital environment.

The birth of 'Medics', however, was not an easy one. Other commitments forced Julia Smith to part company with the project before it reached production; and then her successor, Esta Charkham, worked on just half of the initial series before leaving, too. Gub Neal, then the programme's script editor and busy with his team of writers – Roy Mitchell, Susannah Hagan, Ginnie Hole, John Kerr, Lawrence Gray and Allan Cubitt – was asked by Sally Head to step into the breach and take over the producer's chair.

Gub, who has now become something of a household name as the producer of 'Cracker', put the final touches to the series.

'I wanted it to confront some controversial medical issues,' he says of what has since become a hallmark of the series, 'such as the bigotry of a male-dominated hierarchy, professional malpractice, and the pressures of unrealistic demands on young doctors. Not to mention looking at a number of topical social issues and the behind-the-scenes passions and battles of staff and students alike.'

To ensure the accuracy of his scripts, Gub signed up the series' first medical consultant, Dr David Williams. Although David has moved on, the mantle has passed to his brother John, one of the three present medical consultants.

'That first series of "Medics" provided a pretty irreverent view of an institutionalized profession, as well as giving more than a glimpse into the sex lives of students for which the medical profession is famous,' grins Gub who has well earned his formidable reputation for taking a forthright approach to even the most challenging subjects. 'It did, though, avoid the stark realities of others of its ilk, I think, and in some respects presented a rather more romanticized view of hospital life. Basically, it was a celebration of those launching into the medical profession.'

Much of the first series was filmed on video at several locations in and around Manchester, with the Hope Hospital on Stott Lane, Salford, standing in as the 'Medics' hospital which had been named Henry Park. The concept of the show also provided television debuts for a group of very dissimilar young

Opposite: The winsome Jessica Hardman (Penny Bunton), one of the original students in 'Medics', who qualified as a doctor and appeared in the second and third series.

actors and actresses . . .

The first of these was Penny Bunton, then a twenty-nine-year-old actress from Cambridge, who brought her slender looks and lively personality to the role of Jessica Hardman, a pert, twenty-three-year-old student with a fancy for the opposite sex, and the focus of episode one, 'Jessica's Story'.

In a story liberally sprinkled with sex scenes, Jess had to come to terms with the murder of her married doctor lover whilst in the midst of her studies. She had, in fact, been urged into medicine by her family – in particular her father, Louis Hardman, an eminent consultant

at Henry Park, which added another layer of drama for viewers who tuned in to the very first episode of 'Medics'. Although bright and confident, Jess was obviously never going to match the success of her father in medicine.

'The role was such a challenge,' Penny Bunton recalls today, 'because I had no connections with the medical profession at all. I have always been a bit squeamish, too, so that I was rather apprehensive when they sent me to fol-

Doctors in love: Penny Bunton and Edward Atherton as the star-struck medics who left at the end of the third series to get married.

low this doctor around a major hospital. It was very revealing, though – for they work so *hard!*' (This verdict by the first 'staff member' of 'Medics' has been echoed by virtually every other actor to join the series since.)

Jessica Hardman was Penny's first television role. She had originally been inspired to become an actress at the age of six in a school production in Cambridge. Then after graduating at Oxford, where she enlarged her acting talents, Penny appeared in productions of 'Wuthering Heights' and 'Pygmalion' at the Lyceum Theatre in Edinburgh before being given her big chance in 'Medics'.

'The six of us in that first series of 'Medics' were just thrown together,' she recalls, 'yet we all got on so well. The read-throughs and rehearsals were such fun – I remember giggling a lot while we were doing the scenes in bed – but then I had to film my episode first. I was absolutely scared to death!'

Despite her nerves, Penny became one of the success stories of the original series and remained with 'Medics' as a qualified house officer for series two and three. At the end of this she 'married' fellow student Alex Taylor (now played by Edward Atherton) and left the series to further her career.

The second episode introduced Claire Armstrong, the thirty-four-year-old senior registrar at Henry Park Hospital and tutor to the four students. She was played by Francesca Ryan who was then just beginning what would ulti-mately become an association with

'Medics' spanning four series (See entry in 'Doctors in the House'.)

Claire's character was very much a foretaste of things to come in the series – for she combined a driving ambition to succeed in her chosen profession with the inevitable cost to her personal life. She was also presented as something of a rarity in medicine: a registrar specializing in neuro surgery. Notwithstanding this, Clarie's approachable manner and hard-won expertise made her a popular tutor as well as a sympathetic listener to the problems her students were encounter-ing both within the hospital and in their personal relationships.

Perhaps none of the students had to battle with quite such a severe personal problem as did the Chinese girl with the Mancunian accent, Annie Chung. In episode three, drug-taking reared its ugly head and involved her in a dual struggle for her life and career. Although Annie was still only in her early twenties and lived at home with her parents who ran a successful business, she found it difficult to study at Henry Park and was always ready to kick over the traces.

In fact, the role of Annie, a lively, outspoken and extrovert personality who was popular with her fellow students despite her problems, was tailor-made for twenty-six-year-old Su Lin-Looi with her dazzling smile and burning energy. She also brought to the part an insider's knowledge of the world of medicine.

'My mother is a doctor working in a hospital,' she explains, 'and although my father is actually a lawyer, I have cousins who are in medicine, too.'

Su went into acting by chance. 'I was at boarding school and then went to Leeds University to study English literature,' she explains. 'While I was there I won a scholarship to go to China and spent a year in the country learning all about the Chinese language.'

When she returned to the UK, Su admits, she was broke and out of work,

Francesca Ryan, who played Dr Claire Armstrong, another of the long-running characters in 'Medics'. She finally 'died' in a tragic accident in the fourth series.

but thanks to another cousin who was in the theatre business, she was offered a role at the Riverside Theatre. After that she got herself an agent and won the job fronting Channel Four's programme, 'Orientations'.

'Medics' offered Su Lin-Looi her first taste of TV drama and she threw herself into the role of the troubled student whose best friend is Jessica Hardman with masses of enthusiasm.

'I learned so much on the series,' she says, gratefully. 'About camera technique, about working with professionals. What also made my role as Annie so good was that I was a Chinese girl playing a trainee doctor with the accent on being a medic and not an oriental.'

It was not until episode four that one of the male students moved to centre stage in the series. This was twenty-four-year-old Niall McGuiness – played by Robert Patterson – who came from a poor Irish background and was driven by an all-consuming desire to succeed. Yet in 'Niall's Story', the easy-going charm which he showed to the world was gradually revealed to be masking a deeply-felt insecurity in which he found his working-class background at odds with his education.

Niall had won his place at Henry Park through a Jesuit scholarship. But although he was undoubtedly extremely intelligent, there was also a streak of the opportunist in him. This was seen at work as he wrestled with his conscience over his long-held dream of returning to his southern Irish Catholic roots as a doctor with the greater allure of a high-profile, well-paid job in America.

Speaking of his role, Robert Patterson admits, 'Niall was a likeable lad, but he had a ruthless streak in him.

He really wanted to make it to the top, but all his desire for success made him very intense. He also had a tendency to hypochondria and was always diagnosing himself with one kind of serious illness or another!'

Robert himself is a tousle-haired, uncomplicated man, who differs from Niall in many respects, not least of them the fact that he originates from Belfast, while the student medic's background was south of the border. When he left Ulster for London, Robert's initial ambition was to become an art student, but once in the metropolis he took a post-graduate course at drama school instead.

His early experience was at the Crucible Theatre in Sheffield, following which he directed his energies towards films and TV. He quickly revealed his versatility by playing a 'big, bad cockney' in the Robbie Coltrane-Mel Smith film, 'Nuns on the Run', and then got his first taste of medical life in 'Casualty' in 1989. Robert has subsequently proved to be only the first of several people associated with the BBC's series who have later appeared in 'Medics'.

'The role of Niall really demanded a lot of me as an actor,' he says. 'But the whole show was excellent. The way the cast gelled together so well was incredible. From the time the six of us met up in Manchester for the first read-through we all hit it off immediately. We looked and sounded just like a group of students who had known each other for years.'

He continues, 'Playing an Irishman was actually a bit of a rarity for me – I haven't had to use my accent very often in my career. But Niall was not really like me. He was a far more competitive character and did his best to fit in.'

Episode five of 'Medics' introduced the other qualified doctor, twenty-five-year-old Iraj Irvani, played by Eric Loren, a houseman in the neuro-surgical department of Henry Park. A man of dark, smouldering good looks, he had a nature that switched easily from the arrogant to the humorous.

Iraj was born in Iran, but his artistic family had fled from their homeland at the time of the Revolution and settled in France. He was educated at an English public school, and then after qualifying as a doctor joined the staff of Henry Park where his anglicization was completed.

'Iraj was immensely attractive to women, especially the female medical students, which made him such a terrific role to play,' Eric Loren recalls. 'He used to tease the other medics and he had a superior attitude which was off-putting to some people but still made the women find him strangely magnetic.'

The role actually involved Eric Loren in a complete change of nationality. For he was born in Boston, USA and although determined to follow a career in acting decided against training in either of the nation's two big entertainment centres – New York and Hollywood.

'I came to Britain because I wanted a more classical grounding than modern American acting schools would give me,' he says. 'I wanted to learn every aspect of the business. In fact, the move proved a good thing in more ways than one,

because while I was at drama school I met another student, Carol Starks, and we fell in love and got married.'

After leaving drama school, Eric appeared in repertory in the musical 'Guys and Dolls', had a role in the box office hit, 'Memphis Belle', and then starred as the dentist in a touring production of the very successful grisly comedy 'Little Shop of Horrors'.

As was the case for most of his co-stars, 'Medics' was Eric's first major break on television – though getting the role of Iraj was not without its amusing moments.

'When I first auditioned for the series I sounded like an old Etonian Englishman,' he laughs. 'Then later I was in discussion with the producer and the writers about making the character an American. But in the end I think Iraj really worked well in the overall context of the series.

'Mind you I was terrified of making a mistake when we started filming. I suppose everyone is a bit like that. But in the end it was a terrific role because Iraj had such a lot of different facets to his character.'

Eric particularly enjoyed the scenes he played in Iraj's home – a top-of-the-range flat in the fashionable Arndale Centre in Manchester – which rather contrasted with the house owned by the last member of the 'Medics team', Alex Taylor, in Whalley Range. He shared this with Jessica Hardman and Niall McGuiness which in turn provided the background for some of the most intimate and personal moments experienced by the students away from the hectic pace of Henry Park.

On the surface, Alex Taylor, who was played by Peter Wingfield, seemed to have it all – he was older than the others, gave the impression of being cleverer and seemed destined to succeed. Then suddenly he was faced with the spectre of failure, when he did not pass his final exams, which threatened to deny him the career which all along he had believed to be his right.

Alex was thirty-one, a mature student who had decided to take up medicine after working in the dangerous profession of diver in the North Sea where he had raised the money to fund his training and to purchase the house in Whalley Range.

'He had a very positive attitude towards his career in medicine,' Peter Wingfield reflects. 'But because he was older and thought he knew more than his fellow students he often put on a patronizing manner which the others resented and teased him about.'

That Cardiff-born Peter should have landed his first major television role in 'Medics' is, he still believes today, an amazing coincidence.

'I always wanted to be an actor rather than a doctor,' he says with a wry smile, 'but after three years at Oxford I went to medical school in London. I spent all my spare time with drama groups, and a friend and I actually set up a theatre company. Just three weeks before my finals I decided to quit medicine to concentrate on acting.

'I have to say my family were won-derfully supportive. I enrolled at drama school and this time finished the course in 1989.'

Just a matter of a few weeks later an even bigger surprise awaited Peter when he started to look for work.

'It was amazing. I had no sooner finished drama school than Granada decided to produce this series about medical students. I went along and landed the role of Alex Taylor. I suppose I fitted the bill exactly. So once again I found myself wearing a white coat and being a medical student – the very thing I had tried to get away from!' he laughs.

The coincidences did not quite end there, either. For the writer of the episode in which he appeared was Allan Cubitt who had been a personal friend for years. After finishing work on 'Medics', the rightness of Peter's decision to quit medicine was further underlined when he was offered a role in the BBC production 'The Men's Room' and then got in at the start of what is now another continuing success story – Central TV's series, 'Soldier, Soldier.'

The reactions of viewers and critics to the six-part series were very mixed. Nevertheless, Sally Head decided to give the go-ahead for a second series of 'Medics' – but she wanted to change the focus of the storylines radically. It had already become apparent to the people at Granada that there were severe limitations to stories built around the lives of students and a broader spectrum of hospital life was what was required if the show was to survive.

A new producer, Tony Dennis, was

Peter Wingfield, who actually trained at medical school before appearing in 'Medics' as Alex Taylor.

appointed to mastermind this fresh batch of six, hour-long episodes. He was to prove a good choice, and today Tony enjoys a similar high profile to that of his predecessor, Gub Neal, in the media – his most recent success being that as producer of Kay Mellor's uncompromising drama for Granada about a group of prostitutes, 'Band of Gold', which is also destined for a second series.

'The first series of "Medics" was actually quite a strange mix – sexy and a bit violent,' Tony recalls, 'and it wasn't really about the hospital or medicine. It just happened to pick on four people who were training and the traumas they went through in their lives.'

And so once he had been briefed by Sally Head – who was also acting as executive producer on 'Medics' as well as doing all her other jobs at Granada – Tony set about completely revamping the series. It was decided to concentrate the focus on Henry Park Hospital itself and the people who worked there. Viewers of the first series had undoubtedly become interested in the place – now it was time to reveal much more about what went on both in the wards and behind the closed doors where the doctors and administrators fought their respective battles. To preserve a sense of continuity, three of the most popular characters from 'Medics' 1 were to return: senior registrar Claire Armstrong

plus two of the former students, Jess Hardman, now a house officer, and Alex Taylor who had stalled his career in the last episode as a result of his over-confidence, but was returning to resit his final exams.

Like his predecessor, Tony Dennis decided to give due prominence to a number of topical issues then at the forefront in the world of medicine. The series would also present a striking contrast to other rival medical dramas on TV by taking what he later described as a 'warts and all' approach to hospital life. And to fulfill this ambitious plan, Tony knew that the cast would have to be considerably enlarged with some well-known faces coming in place of the other young actors who had launched 'Medics'.

Reflecting on the overall concept of the programme at that point in its history, Tony Dennis says, 'The idea was that our characters were in a pressure-cooker environment. They were not always going to be nice to patients – they would even make jokes about them behind their backs. They were people who got rattled and didn't necessarily treat each other as considerately as they should. But that's all very understandable. Because if you're working 150 hours a week, you're not disposed to being particularly nice all the time!'

The transfused 'Medics' was also intending to throw a revealing light on to the normally unseen men and women who have the difficult job of running a hospital: those in administration and finance.

Tony Dennis explains the thinking behind this new element of the series. 'What it comes down to is the fact that, at a time of increasing demands on the NHS, there are numerous hospitals suffering great cuts in their resources. Henry Park is just such a place and like all the rest, the people running it have to do the best they can within the present political climate. Arguably, it's a matter of survival for perhaps our most valued institution.'

Three scriptwriters, Sam Snape, Kevin Hood and Jacqueline Holborough, then set to work with the new script editor, Fiona Howe, to create six episodes which between them tackled the subjects of AIDS, breast cancer, multiple sclerosis, gangland violence, the use of resources for terminally ill patients, the demands of research against the requirements of patient care, litigation over alleged negligence – not forgetting the problems of professional ambition and personal trauma among the medical staff themselves.

Into this varied mix of storylines were brought the characters – and the actors to play them – who would ultimately do most to ensure the series's popularity and who have, almost without exception, continued in their roles to the present fifth series. Their complementary nature and the skill with which they have worked together in bringing the medics to life is also a tribute to casting director, Sarah Bird.

Unquestionably the most visible of all was Tom Baker, forever remembered as the larger-than-life fourth Doctor Who, cast as Professor Geoffrey Hoyt, Henry Park's equally flamboyant consultant in General Surgery with an eccentric approach to both his work and to other people. Of equal stature was Sue Johnston, known to millions for her role in the long-running soap, 'Brookside', signed to play Ruth Parry, the general manager, who would soon become known as the 'Iron Lady of Henry Park' because of her ambitious plans to raise the profile of the hospital.

Among the other faces who would also rapidly become familiar to viewers were James Gaddas as the charismatic senior registrar, Dr Robert Nevin; Emma Cunningham playing the attractive senior house officer, Dr Gail Benson; Hugh Quarshie as Dr Tom Carey, the ambitious research consultant in neurology; Teddie Thompson as Alison Makin, a final year student destined to become a house officer on the chest ward; and Jimmi Harkishin as the dedicated Dr Jay Rahman also destined to become a registrar. (The careers of all of these are discussed in 'Doctors in the House').

The decision to make 'Medics' a more hospital-based series meant that Tony and his team headed by production manager Mick Graham had to find more suitable locations for the various wards, special care units, operating theatres and administration offices required

Opposite: Dr Claire Armstrong (Francesca Ryan) was always struggling with the demands of her work and the needs of her husband Gavin (Ian Ferguson) during her time at Henry Park.

Left: Hugh Quarshie played Research Consultant Dr Tom Carey, who allowed his ambition to cloud his judgement.

Below: A publicity photograph of the whole 'Medics' cast, taken during the filming of the third series.

by the storylines.

'There were quite a few NHS hospitals in and around Manchester that had a spare ward or two available,' Tony recalls, 'but not enough in any one of them for us to be able to film everything in one place. So after a lot of scouting around we ended up using four different hospitals and a number of houses as the doctors' homes.'

Probably Tony's most vital decision was picking the hospital to be used as the exterior of the mythical Henry Park. The final decision was made in favour of Tameside General in Fountain Street, Ashton-under-Lyme because it was felt that its architectural appearance, ranging as it does from the Victorian era to the present day, would enable the team to use different kinds of interior scenes from other hospitals which would not seem out of place behind such a frontage. The interior scenes then alternated between Hope Hospital which had already been used in the first series, Trafford General in Manchester, and Prestwich Hospital which had the best facilities for operating theatre scenes, if the grimmest environment.

The crew members who worked on the second series – and the two which followed – remember their lives as being rather like that of a 'travelling circus'. The cavalcade of buses, lorries, trucks, mobile caravans and cars which were needed to carry the filming and technical equipment to the location as well as the actors' mobile changing rooms, make-up and props department, had to be driven virtually every day from the centre of Manchester to wherever the location might be.

Stories about the so-called 'glamour' of making television drama series inevitably bring a rueful smile to the faces of members of a film crew, the cameramen, sound recordists, grips, gaffers, chargehands, joiners, painters and the rest – and of none is this more true than of those who worked on the early series of 'Medics'. For not only did they face all the demands of setting up scenes before the actors arrived on call – an operation that often started as early as 7 am and did not finish until twelve hours later (see typical CALL SHEET reprinted on pages 127 and 128) – but also facing the problems of not disturbing the daily routine of the rest of the hospital.

Several of the longer-serving crew members vividly remember having to wear medics' 'blues' over their ordinary clothes whenever they were filming in working hospitals. A number of the actors also found themselves in the amusing situation of being addressed as 'Doctor' as they hurried in white coats from make-up to the day's location in several of the buildings. Production staff also regularly had to redirect patients who strayed into a ward where filming was taking place mistaking the rows of 'extras' occupying beds for the real thing.

Recording the soundtrack also produced its special headaches. Untoward noises from elsewhere in the hospital such as the simple squeak of a trolley being moved about, builders working on the roof of the premises or an aircraft heading for Manchester Airport, all could also abort a scene time and again.

Transporting the stars and extras from their homes or the hotels where they were staying in and around Manchester provided another exercise in logistics that an Army platoon officer would have admired. The provision of three meals a day – breakfast, lunch and an afternoon break for tea and sandwiches – was another essential part of the operation for a hungry group of cast and crew numbering anything from an average of thirty-seven crew and a dozen artistes to a figure nearing the hundred mark when large numbers of extras were required.

But these special problems in the filming of 'Medics' also brought the cast and crew closer together, making them feel almost like a family – a feeling which is still evident today in the easy familiarity which exists between everyone associated with the series. An underlying sense of humour often eases the tensest situation, and as television people on both sides of the camera are renowned practical jokers, the occasional bit of fun or ribald remark is as much a part of the day's routine as the director's call for 'Action!'

By the time Tony Dennis began working on the third series, the main characters on the staff of Henry Park had been firmly established in viewers' minds and were quite clearly growing in popularity as was evidenced by Granada's increasing postbag and in the reviews of newspaper critics. With the blessing of Sally Head, another six episodes took this development a stage further.

The contemporary debate about the state of the NHS was, once again, reflected in the scripts – by Kevin Hood (2), Alison Fisher, Andy Smith and Peter Bowker (2) – along with a number of intense professional battles and the interplay of various personal emotions. Among the topics explored in this series

were leukemia, brain damage, the trial of new drugs, resources and sponsorship and, all the time, the pressing need to provide better care for patients. Changes also occurred to Henry Park Hospital itself when it became a Trust.

However, at the centre of the storyline was the compelling relationship between Geoffrey Hoyt and Ruth Parry. The two principals had been drawn together in the previous series as a result of a threat of litigation following a gynaecological operation that had gone wrong. But the alliance was still an uneasy one.

Ruth, as the general manager, was even more determined to run the hospital as a successful enterprise despite the competitive pressures in the medical marketplace. In the midst of this, she suddenly found herself having to face a crisis when a deficit of £12million in the hospital's finaces was uncovered. Hoyt, now also on the board with her, was revealed as a man committed to ensuring that Henry Park got the funding it deserved though not always seeing eye to eye over just *where* the need was greatest. At the climax to the series, he, too, faced a crisis when it was revealed that he had an ailing wife whom even his great skills could not save. Indeed, her death in the last episode left him so distressed that he was involved in a terrible car accident.

The series also featured a plan to split the medical school from the hospital – which, after strong protests, was dropped – plus the opening of a new cardiac unit and the mounting of a campaign for a liver transplant unit.

Elsewhere in the medical hierarchy the pressures and rewards of the job gave certain members of the staff cause to think about their career moves, while for others it was just a matter of continuing to struggle through each day as best they could.

Claire Armstrong, who lost her bid for the consultancy vacancy now occupied by Dr Tom Carey, completed some ethically delicate research while at the same time being torn between two men: her lover, Dr Robert Nevin, and her husband, Gavin, the father of her unborn child. Carey, for his part, had his ambitious sights set on the chair of neurology and perhaps the even bigger prize of a future in America. And watching all these events with more than a little interest was house officer Gail Benson: herself involved in a dilemma about her future prospects and an ever deepening relationship with Dr Nevin. Jay Rahman, at least, had done his career prospects nothing but good by making an inspired diagnosis about a patient with jaundice, and now sensed that perhaps membership of the Royal College of Physicians might finally be just around the corner for him . . .

The cliff-hangers in the third series stretched throughout all the corridors of power in Henry Park and set up the fourth series intriguingly for the summer of 1994 – once Granada had decided to

give it the go-ahead. Before it reached the screen, however, Tony Dennis handed over the producer's role to Alison Lumb – a lady who already had a remarkable association with medical series on television.

In television terms, 'Medics' had up to this point in time been 'building an audience'. Sally Head now felt ready to capitalize on its achievements by increasing the number of episodes from six to ten, although still retaining its summer spot in the broadcasting schedules. The task of making this quantum leap was offered to Alison Lumb who had previously been at the BBC – most relevantly on the Corporation's own medical drama series, 'Casualty'.

'I had worked on the fourth and fifth series of "Casualty" and been the script editor on the third series of "House of Eliott" when Granada made me the offer to produce "Medics" in the autumn of 1993,' the attractive and energetic Alison recalls. 'The plan was to shoot the series from 8 November to 23 April and complete the editing by the end of June for transmission in July.

'I thought "Casualty" had been a baptism of fire. But that was until I joined "Medics"! I suppose I hesitated for about ten seconds over the schedule, asking myself, "Is this possible?"'

Deciding to accept the challenge – 'in the tenth second' – Alison immediately found herself in a unique position. No one before in television had moved from a major medical series on one channel to another. Despite all the pressure she knew she would have to face,

Opposite: A moment of tranquillity for Ruth Parry and Geoffrey Hoyt at his farm, filmed at Agden Bridge, Lymm.

Alison instantly believed that having ten episodes at her disposal was a considerable advantage over just six.

'What I had inherited was a series of complex characters working in a stressful environment. They were not cosy and reassuring people and I knew we would have to add some more of the same ilk. Ten episodes would give them all a lot more room in which to breathe.'

Alison is very ready to counter any suggestions that 'Medics' is in any way the same as 'Casualty' – excpet that they are both about medical life.

'"Medics" is not like "Casualty" where you are dealing with four or five episodic stories, and the main characters are always likely to walk on and administer medicine. This series is not didactic.

'Of course both series put a lot of painstaking research into the scripts. But "Medics" view of hospital life is very different because it roams much further than just the Accident and Emergency departments.'

While she was employed as the scriopt editor of 'Casualty', Alison says she got very used to 'creating scripts whose pace and energy stood up on their own'. What, though, she liked about 'Medics' was the opportunity to introduce music.

'This was quite a change for me,' she reflects. 'I had to get used to using music that was supportive of the action and underlined the emotions of those involved. "Medics" was also different in that it was shot on film rather than the tape which had been used in "Casualty".

'Tape is a significant factor in making a series more gritty,' she explains. 'But film has a less documentary and more of a feature-film feeling about it. To get to the grittiness you have to fight against its natural sumptuousness.'

When it came to broadening the scope of the series and introducing new characters, Alison worked closely with Louise Berridge who had joined her as script editor.

'We sat down and looked at the strengths that were already there in "Medics", she recalls. 'Then we decided to bring a rigour to the structure of the stories. I was also keen to increase the number of independent female characters. Women who are motivated from within. Not just someone who is somebody's colleague, wife or girlfriend.'

To the cast of 'regulars' – Tom Baker, Sue Johnston, James Gaddas, Hugh Quarshie, Francesca Ryan, Emma Cunningham, Jimmi Harkishin, and Teddie Thompson – the new producer and her associate introduced the senior consultant in plastics, Helen Lomax (Dinah Stabb); senior registrar Dr Sarah Kemp (Patricia Kerrigan); resources manager, Derek Foster (Nick Dunning); and charge nurse Billy Cheshire played by Clarence Smith.

Alison also decided to put more focus on those who were on the receiving end of the Medics' many and varied

Opposite: The attractive Helen Lomax (Dinah Stabb), the senior consultant in plastic surgery, started out as Professor Hoyt's doctor but soon became closer to him.

skills and emotions – the patients.

'I wanted the patients to be fully fleshed characters. Not just bodies in beds. That way we could get to know them, care about their stories and give the doctors, nurses and administrators a chance to interact with their problems.'

The result was a number of guest artists who started appearing in series four and have continued in five. One of the first of these long-term patients was Julie Coleman (Judy Brooke). She remained for six of the episodes during which her condition provided a whole new element of interest for regular viewers to the series.

'Julie gave us a great opportunity to evolve a relationship between a doctor – Dr Robert Nevin – and a patient who was suffering from the life-threatening dangers of hepatitis B and cirrhosis of the liver. But I didn't want the character to descend into bathos. Even though she was usually lying flat in bed or sitting in a wheelchair, I wanted her to have a sparkiness that would make viewers really care about her.

'When we came to cast the part I remembered Judy from when she had appeared as the perky babysitter in 'The Beiderbecke Affair'. She was just right – even though she was bright yellow for most of the series and we had to do some horrible medical things to her!'

Among the other 'guest patients'

Ruth Parry (Sue Johnston) confronted Dr Tom Carey about the ethics of his research during the fourth series and was horrified by what she discovered.

who appeared in the Henry Park wards during the fourth series were Helen Baxendale (as Fran Newland) and burns victim Adam Wood (played by Michael Blake).

The main storylines of Alison's fourth season were a controversy over a Bosnian war hero, a trial for manslaughter, a comedy of errors over sexual orientation and a major house fire leading to a racist attack at Henry Park.

On the personal front, Professor Hoyt returned to Henry Park after being involved in the car accident which had directly resulted from his wife's death. This showed him to be a man having difficulty in coming to terms with both his physical and emotional scars. At the hospital, however, he unexpectedly found consolation from Helen Lomax the tough and determined new plastic surgeon who started out merely treating his injuries but gradually got underneath his emotional guard.

Ruth Parry also found herself wrestling with her conscience when she learned that Tom Carey's drug research was flawed and the huge payment from the American company Heisenberg which would come as such a god-send to Henry Park was under threat. Then came the revelation that Carey had stolen research work from Claire Armstrong's notes, which heralded Hugh Quarshie's decision to leave the series. For Ruth Parry herself, a period of respite when she went on sabbatical only allowed the ambitious new resources manager Derek Foster to begin undermining her position.

The departure of Tom Carey was not, however, the only one by a member of the staff of Henry Park in series four. Claire Armstrong who had managed to keep her marriage intact despite an affair with Dr Nevin, insisted on attending a welcome back party for Geoffrey Hoyt and at the climax of the first episode fell down a flight of stairs to her death. With the 'demise' of Claire, 'Medics' lost its longest-serving member of the original cast.

Ambition was Gail Benson's driving force during the fourth series as she pursued her desire to become a surgeon,

The professional and private relationship between Drs Gail Benson (Emma Cunningham) and Jay Rahman (Jimmi Harkishin) has rollercoastered throughout their time together in 'Medics'.

while Dr Jay Rahman, for all his undoubted commitment to medicine, nursed a far more basic desire for the pretty house officer. And for Dr Alison Makin, after struggling to come to terms with her sexuality during the two previous series – not to mention a fling with Jay – there was the arrival of senior registrar Sarah Kemp who might just have been the lover she had been seeking all the time . . .

The strands of drama and emotional involvement which once again highlighted the series were no mean achievement for the production team who had worked under such pressure – as they were also a credit to the ten scriptwriters: Tony Etchells, Rosamund Orde-Powlett, Robin Mukherjee, Sarah Daniels, Philip Myall, Steve Trafford, Andy Smith, Neil McKay, David Richard-Fox and Sam Snape.

All this time, as Alison Lumb worked with her team and advisers and grew ever closer to the world of medicine, her admiration and appreciation for those in it increased enormously.

'They are saviours – knights on white chargers,' she says, simply. 'But they are also people working under great stress. Doctors can certainly be egotistical. There is undoubtedly an arrogance to the professional ethos. We automatically have interesting characters, but there's also endless story potential. All human life is in "Medics" – all genders, all races.'

Alison is in no doubt, though, that there are some viewers who turn on programmes about hospital life for what she calls their 'gore quotient'.

'But what I believe people really go for is characters who are in crisis. And that crisis can either be a consequence of a lifetime's behaviour or something that has just happened. But whichever it is, they have reached a point of crisis where decisions have to be made.'

These words were to prove uncannily prophetic for Alison Lumb herself. For such was the strain of producing the fourth series, that she was not well enough to return to Manchester when shooting of the fifth series was approved in early 1995. Her contribution to 'Medics' was undeniable, though – her bold decisions had finally made the show a ratings winner. In television terms, it had 'taken off'.

Although she is no longer in charge, Alison's thoughts have often been with the cast and crew as they worked through the summer of 1995 to film 'Medics' 5 – now increased to twelve episodes and booked for a prime-time spot in the autumn schedules.

And so it is that 'Medics' – which began its life as the handiwork of a small group who thought of themselves jokingly as a kind of 'travelling circus' – is now an established hit with audiences throughout the British Isles. Now, too, it has its own 'home' quite unlike that enjoyed by any other medical series – a once barred and shuttered hospital that has come alive again thanks to the magic of television . . .

THE WORLD OF
HENRY PARK

THE SOLID, RED-BRICK EDI-FICE that is Ancoats Hospital on Old Mill Street has been a landmark on the eastern flank of Manchester for over a century. Built in 1888, the hospital with its four floors of wards, operating theatres, special-care units and rather barrack-like administrative offices all draped with iron escape staircases and grouped around a central quadrangle, was a focal point in the region's medical care until it was closed down in 1994.

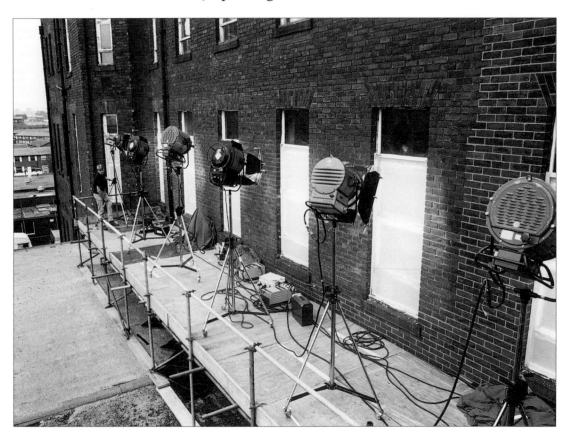

The recently-closed Ancoats Hospital in Old Mill Street, Manchester, may look much the same on the outside, but inside (above) it was transformed into Henry Park Hospital, as now being seen in the fifth series.

Only a recently built single-storey outpatients department and community health clinic, attached to the original ornate Victorian main entrance block with its shuttered sash windows and crowned chimneys is still in use each day except for Sunday.

But for the intervention of fate in the form of a television company looking for a home for its medical drama series, Ancoats might today still be a derelict and decaying monument to health care in the city as well as being one more symbol of the demands of government policy. For it is here that the Granada production team are filming the fifth series of Medics after four years of utilizing hospital facilities at a number of different locations around the city.

Ancoats Hospital – or the Ardwick and Ancoats Dispensary as the legend in gothic lettering around the arch of the boarded-up front door proclaims – stands on a landscape of derelict factories, offices and shops, only relieved by a group of new superstores on Great Ancoats Street. Although only the outpatients department is functioning, a sign on the main road still indicates the hospital's whereabouts, while those who live in an adjacent council estate remember the flurry of activity when it was learned that the building was earmarked for a major role treating casualties from the Falklands War. When these never materialized, it was mothballed.

The unique decision to make the series almost wholly within the walls of a real hospital was not only a brave one, but one which required an enormous amount of pre-planning and work before a single scene could be filmed. Taking a guided tour of the facility – as I did recently – it is possible to get some idea of the transformation that the men and women employed on the project created during the winter of 1994-5. Prior to that, entering the complex felt, in the words of one of the team who was there the entire time, 'like taking a step back into the cold, dank days of Victorian England at its grimmest'.

Although the only part of the complex that members of the general public enter today is the modest but efficient out-patients department and community health clinic, the hospital itself was for years one of the jewels in the crown of industrial Manchester with an important history of medical achievement amidst all the grim realities of life in a big city.

The Ashton Canal which runs behind the hospital and under a bridge at Great Ancoats Street has also long been notorious for a double murder that took place there on 10 May 1812, when a militiaman, John Moore, and a female relative were murdered as they walked home at midnight after drinking at the nearby Kings Arms. Although a cry of 'Murder!' quickly went up from a number of other late-night passers-by and several men were seen running from the scene of the crime, no one was ever apprehended, despite the offer of a reward of £200. It was not, in fact, until the following morning that the bodies of the unfortunate Moore and his relative were even discovered floating in the grimy canal.

Shortly after this, in 1820, the original Ardwick and Ancoats Dispensary was opened in what was then the city's bustling and overcrowded factory and tenement district, and a surgeon named Dr James Kay began his work among local people – many of whom were suffering terribly from dysentery and flu. It was here that Dr Kay developed his theory of the connection between ill-health and poor environment and it was his pioneer investigations into sanitary conditions and the damage which was being done to people's health by defective drainage, that first put the name of Ancoats on the medical map.

Following the construction of the present building in 1888 – and its opening by Prince Albert – Ancoats again became the location of another piece of medical history. For within its walls Manchester-born Dr Alfred Ernest Barclay set up his first primitive appara-

Opposite: Terry Reeve, Production Manager of 'Medics', who has played a key role in the creation of the new world of Henry Park.

44

tus to investigate the new and exciting science of radiology. Although Barclay subsequently moved to the Royal Infirmary when it was opened in 1908, and there established a first-class radiology department which proceeded to make notable advances in the radiology of the alimentary tract and won for him an international reputation, he never forgot the encouragement he had received in Ancoats. Nor has popular legend forgotten the stories of his fragile glass globes and machinery which were said to be 'forever surrounded by zones of profanity' . . .

The man who initiated the re-opening of Ancoats for the filming of 'Medics', production manager, Terry Reeve, knew something of the hospital's history, but sensed more strongly that here might just be what the rapidly developing series needed to fulfill yet another demanding Spring and Summer shooting schedule.

Terry, a quietly-spoken man whose gentle demeanour belies a fierce determination and careful eye for detail, explains what first attracted him to the then-derelict building and its locality.

'On the previous series we had been just like a group of New Age travellers,' he says 'moving about from one location to another in a ramshackle collection of vehicles for costumes, props, cameras, lighting, catering and the actors. But finding somewhere that had been a hospital I felt we could spend three out of each of the four weeks it takes to film two episodes back to back in the facility, and then just one week on the road

shooting any location scenes such as the doctors' homes, the pub where they meet, even Professor Hoyt's farm.'

Terry also hoped that having the hospital location might just make his job a little less problematical – although he explains his function on the series with a modesty that belies its complexity and importance to the success of 'Medics'.

'I basically spend the money that the producer has battled with Granada to get to make the series,' he smiles. 'There are obviously plenty of other people who spend the budget. But it is my global responsibility to keep 'Medics' on budget and on time. Guiding everybody along. We have regular financial meetings every four weeks after each block of filming to see how things are going. I suppose you could say I am directly responsible for really everything and anything.'

Anyone who spends any time with Terry as he goes about his daily tasks in the now-refurbished vastness of the hospital, in the Granada offices or even on location, soon comes to appreciate just what that means.

It is interesting to learn that, ideal as Ancoats seems for its purpose, the series might well not have been using it if certain other things had worked out differently. Again Terry explains.

'For the last series we shot quite a lot of scenes in the Salford Royal Hospital. It was actually a very small hospital in comparison to the big hospitals which are in operation today. But when the Salford Area Health Authority became a national health trust last year, the owernship of the hospital ceded to the regional health authority who decided they didn't want it hanging around their necks and promptly put it on the market for sale.

'That was when we first seriously thought about getting our own hospital. But as soon as we started talking to the authority about renting the hospital they were not prepared to take it off the market for the duration of the filming. Obviously we couldn't start production with the possibility that the place might be sold out from underneath us.'

Terry smiles wryly at the memory of what might have been. But the germ of an idea had been sown and had begun to take root in the production team's thinking – especially when the possibility of Ancoats being available came up.

'Ancoats had been empty for about a year when we first had a look,' he continues. 'I remember my first impression was how big it was – how much space there would be for all those complex scenes which are part of everyday life in a busy hospital. We also found that the fabric was still fairly well maintained and there were no obvious signs of any major structural faults.

'The out-patients and community health clinic at the front of the building were still open and functioning normally from Monday to Saturday. But the rest was closed off and with the quadrangle between the out-patients and the main building barred from public access we had all the space we needed for parking essential vehicles such as the catering truck and transport vans and minibuses.'

Once the decision had been made by Granada to hire Ancoats for the year, the real work for Terry and his production team began. The memory can still give him a little shiver.

'We didn't move in until last winter,' he says. 'The place had been closed down some time earlier and so all the water supplies had been drained. There was dust and damp everywhere. Cobwebs festooned the wards, dirt lay inches deep in the operating theatres, and there were piles of old beds and pieces of equipment stacked everywhere. It was still possible to see it had been a hospital, but it looked like something out of Dickens. Somebody even told us it was supposed to be haunted.'

Indeed, Ancoats *is* haunted – not by one ghost, but two. According to several accounts subsequently relayed to the Granada team, the ghost of a matron who once worked in one of the top-floor wards has been seen floating by a window on a number of occasions. While the second tale records the facts about a nurse who was said to have hanged herself on one of the wards when all the pressures of tending to the sick and dying became too much for her . . .

But it was not these stories that most chilled Terry Reeve.

'If you remember, last winter was particularly cold. When we first entered the building it was like walking into a freezer. The whole place seemed so inhospitable – if you'll excuse the pun and depressing. I think for a while some people even began to wonder if we had done the right thing.

'But it is amazing what difference putting on a bit of heat can make. As soon as we got the heating going, the whole place took on a warmer personality. Then when we got busy with a lick of paint here and a lick of paint there, everything took on a whole new feeling. It was as if the hospital was coming back to life again – which in a way, of course, it was.'

The water system also had to be put back on – which created its own problems, too.

'It was just one of the many things we had to cope with,' Terry reminisces. 'The pipes had to be refilled and we had to make sure that everything was watertight and running properly. We might not have been planning to have real patients in the wards, but that cut no ice with the health authority. They insisted that we took full responsibility for making sure the water moved around the system regularly. They were very worried about any possibility of an outbreak of legionnaire's disease. Even while we were still shivering from the cold we were told to make sure all the fire extinguishers were working properly.'

The production team also had to take care not to do any work on the structure of the hospital without getting the proper permission. Terry's constant nightmare was of an official from the town hall turning up and demanding to know why a particular wall had been knocked down.

'I kept hearing this voice replying, "Well, we didn't think you'd mind?" and then the curt response: "Well, I do – put it back!"'

Opposite: A typical emergency scene being filmed for 'Medics', with Gail Benson (Emma Cunningham) and Robert Nevin (James Gaddas) appearing against a backdrop of authentically awful hospital curtains.

One of Terry's major concerns from the start was to ensure that the interior of the Henry Park which would be appearing in the fifth series was not too dissimilar to the one that had been seen earlier.

'What we decided to do when we moved in here after using the various locations last year where the style of the front of the building dictated what each ward looked like, was not to make too many dramatic changes again. Having used four different hospitals already, it would have been a monumental leap for the viewer following the series if the style had changed all over again. So rather than do that to them, we set out to utilize the wards in Ancoats to create as much of the same impression as they did last year.'

Terry cites two of the most difficult problems he faced in this respect. 'Probably the hardest to overcome was the burns unit. Because the one we utilized at Salford Royal was actually a corridor with rooms off it! It wasn't actually an open ward – there was a very small office at one end – and it had a very distinctive style about it. So what we have done at Ancoats is use a ground-floor ward which has three bays and four beds – and closed one of these off and made it into an office. We've also decorated it in the same style to give it the visual feel of its predecessor. So you can see we have

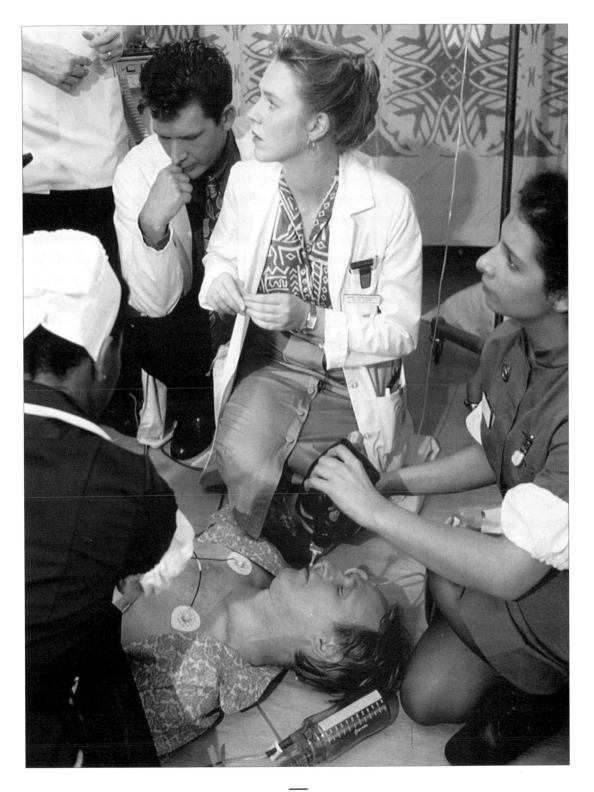

tried hard to make it look similar to what everybody remembers from last year – while at the same time making it a bit easier to move the cameras around.'

The general medical ward in which a large number of scenes take place was also something of a headache to convert.

'When Ancoats was a real hospital the actual ward office was on the opposite side of the corridor going into the ward. But this was completely wrong as far as the office in Henry Park was concerned. And to make matters worse, it was *tiny* – it would have been impossible to film in it!

'What we did find in the right spot was a two-bedded side ward. So Chris Wilkinson, our art director, who was responsible for the set-up of the whole place decided to split this in half and put in a false wall. This gave us a walled office big enough to shoot in. But it didn't have any windows overlooking the ward like the previous one. So that's when we decided to open up the wall and put in two new panes of glass to give the same impression.'

However, Terry took no risk of a difficult visit by the man from the local authority by fully disclosing the idea.

'We soon discovered that a number of parts of Ancoats are listed,' he explains, 'and so when we did things like adding windows or taking cladding from the stairs – anything that might be considered contentious – we went straight to the listed buildings officer and building control officer and I'm glad to say they were quite happy to give us permission.'

As the steady thump of hammers and the sweep of paint brushes brought Ancoats gradually back to life in anticipation of the arrival of the camera crew and actors, Terry was delighted to see another of his objectives being realized. By abandoning all the travelling and setting-up costs of the previous series, he had now freed money from the budget for other equally vital expenses.

'Because we were no longer going to have to be on the road for three out of every four weeks, I was able to make some of that money available for hidden costs, such as the lighting and heating of Ancoats, which we have to pay for on top of the fee for the use of the hospital; and also for setting up two production offices, rooms for costume storage, make-up, and an actors' green room. And all of this courtesy of what had previously been a basically redundant, derelict and shut-down building!'

When the various wards, special units and offices of the fictional Henry Park Hospital were ready, Terry Reeve's final task before shooting began was to acquire the medical equipment for use in the episodes. Here the present government's policy of closing down a large number of hospitals in recent months proved a windfall for 'Medics'.

'The closure of so many hospitals has meant that there is quite a market for second-hand equipment,' Terry states.

Bedside manners on the ward: Charge Nurse Billy Cheshire (Clarence Smith) and Dr Jay Rahman (Jimmi Harkishin) caring for a seriously ill patient with the help of some borrowed equipment.

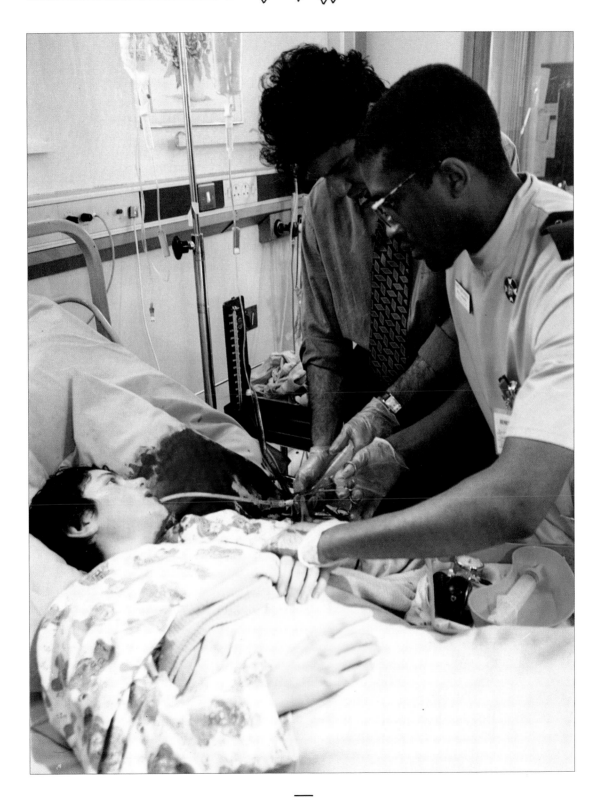

'For example, two hospitals in Liverpool recently closed and our production buyer went over there and was able to get hold of quite a stock of beds and bedside cabinets – all that sort of thing – which were redundant. This means that we can be reasonably modern and up to date, though they are not the very latest, state of the art pieces of furniture which most hospitals now have.'

Much of the consumable equipment used on the series, Terry says with a smile, he usually 'begs, borrows or steals' from hospitals or medical suppliers.

'Sometimes it is just not possible to get into a hospital to film a particular piece of specialist equipment. That's when we contact the manufacturers and see if there is a demonstraction model free and someone who can set it up and show us how to use it.

'Of course, we have to be careful about advertising and trade names, but in the medical field there are so few major manufacturers that this is not generally a problem. Because we always try to be realistic in everything we show on 'Medics', if there is a piece of equipment already in use in the NHS for a particular diagnosis we are featuring, then this is the one we *must* have.'

Among the specialist pieces of equipment that Terry is particularly pleased to have featured in the series was a CT Scanner at Tameside Hospital. 'The scanner was obviously something we couldn't bring out of the hospital, but we were delighted to have the opportunity to go in and film it there.'

The North Manchester Health Care Trust, the owners of Ancoats, have also put a lot of their technical facilities and contacts at the call of Terry Reeve and his team.

'They have been especially helpful with detail – things like curtains, bedding and all that sort of stuff which is unique to hospitals,' says Terry. 'If you went out and tried to purchase the curtains, for instance, you wouldn't be able to buy anything so gross! [laughs]. The curtains even have their own pattern book, and being for hospital use they have to be fire-proof. At first we investigated getting some made for us, but because they would have had to be made to such a high standard in terms of cloth, it was actually cheaper for us to make them ourselves from a less fire-resistant material. We didn't need to be so exact – we are not a real hospital after all! But most of the things seen in the series are genuine – there is just no way of codding it.'

The makers of 'Medics' are also too conscious of the fact that certain viewers take a delight in studying everything that appears on the screen and are quick to write and point out anything that is not authentic. Terry delights in telling one story which proves the obverse of this fact.

'In an earlier series we had a story about a dialysis unit,' he says. 'In order to film this we got hold of some obsolete kidney machines from Hope Hospital and set them up in an empty ward at Trafford Hospital. They had apparently been out of operation for some months and been left standing in a corridor. They were ultimately destined to go to

Russia for cannibalizing for spares. It seems that although we [in the NHS] are using state of the art kidney equipment about three generations on from these, in Russia they are still front-line equipment.

'In any event, we arranged the loan of these kidney machines for a few days and Hope sent us one of their technicians to get them running again. Now while all this was going on, some medical students at Trafford saw that we were setting up a dialysis machine and wrote a letter of protest to the local press. "Why is this TV company being allowed to use valuable machines?" they demanded to know, "when people are queuing up, some of them dying, because they can't get kidney treatment!" And what they were actually talking about was machinery that had been thrown out as being *redundant*.'

Terry says that this is not the only time that 'Medics' has been accused of using equipment that has 'been taken away from patients'. In response, he assures everyone, 'Most of the items like those kidney machines which we use are actually redundant or spare to capacity. It is possible they might be what a hospital would use normally, but they just haven't got the space or personnel to use them. Which is how they come to be on loan to us. 'Medics' is certainly *not* in the business of taking much-needed equipment away from sick patients!'

Now that the production team are happily settled in the revamped Ancoats they would be more than happy to stay there if and when a sixth series is made.

'I think I can safely say this is an excellent home for us,' Terry says. 'We would certainly like to stay. But that will depend on the out-patients department and whether North Manchester Health Care Trust want to keep it running. If they closed it down it would be a different matter for us.'

In fact, the series takes advantage of the one day of the week that this unit is shut – Sunday – for filming the arrival of 'accidents' and 'emergencies' at the fictional Henry Park.

'That's the actual purpose it served when the whole of Ancoats was still open,' Terry explains, 'which is why it has a ramp at the front that's absolutely invaluable to us.'

Having at last walked through the maze of corridors inside Ancoats that now hum with life once again, it is easy to appreciate the size of the task Terry Reeve and the other behind-the-scenes members of the ' Medics' team have achieved.

'Because the building was derelict it was almost like starting up an entirely new hospital,' Terry reflects. 'Now that it is functioning as we want it to, it is perhaps not quite so demanding as having to run a real hospital. But it is certainly *getting* that way.'

Wouldn't it be ironic, I suggested to the production manager, as we completed our tour outside the general ward where the day's filming was about to begin, if having allowed Ancoats to be revived the Health Care Trust now decided to reopen it?

'Well, a few weeks ago we had a visit

from the Lord Mayor of Manchester and among the members of his party was the chairman of the Trust. Neither of them had seen the place since we had moved in and we got the distinct impression they were impressed. Ian Fowler, who is the press officer of the Trust, was particularly intrigued by what we had done with the old phsyiotherapy area – although it took him a few moments to realize just where he was. For the room is now the Henry Park canteen.

'Ian told me that the last time he had been in the building before it was closed down the room had been a 'bed graveyard' – just about every old bed that had broken down in the hospital was stored there along with lots of old pieces of derelict equipment. In fact, it had been so full of junk it had been virtually impossible to get in. Now the room was a bright, cheerful canteen, complete with steaming cookers and trays of food. He was so stunned I was almost sorry to have to tell him that both the steam and the mouth-watering dishes on display were actually artificial!'

Terry left to return to the many jobs which face him each day as he works hard to keep his hospital within a hospital functioning. He paused to make one last comment, sweeping his arm in the direction of the general ward.

'In Henry Park there are supposed to be about 850 beds,' he smiled, 'and each one has its own story. Sounds a bit like 'The Naked City', doesn't it – and think how long *that* series lasted!'

A BURNING MATTER

Perhaps the most spectacular stunt seen in 'Medics' was the burning of a home belonging to an Asian family in the fourth series which was filmed in the Spring of 1994 and screened on 29 August of that year. The fire provided the background to a major burns story in which a number of people were killed and several badly injured. Although the blaze was initially thought to have been caused by a faulty heater in a ground-floor flat belonging to an old woman with a penchant for looking after stray cats, it was ultimately revealed to be an arson attack directed at the Asians by an extreme right-wing organization.

To find a location that looked habitable but could also be seen convincingly on fire tested all the resources of the 'Medics' special effects team. Their search to find a suitable building took them all over the Manchester area until finally a terrace of four houses was found in Hyde. The property was in the middle of an Urban Renewal Area and was due for imminent demolition. The only

A fire engine stands by during the filming of the blazing house episode for 'Medics'.

problem, however, was that there was still one tenant refusing to move from the end house. He was an Asian and was objecting to being turned out because it was then the middle of Ramadan.

The 'Medics' production team naturally liaised with Tameside Council about the planned fire – not only in order to discuss any possible dangers, but also because of the storyline featuring a minority racial group. In fact, the episode could not have been more topical because there had actually been a series of such incidents in the local Asian community during previous years which obviously saved the Granada team from accusations of inciting fire raising.

The controlled blaze was duly filmed on a night shoot, with the local fire brigade in close attendance, and made for a dramatic sequence in the series. However, for those who worked on the fire scenes – both members of the film crew and actors – the most enduring memory was not of the fictional drama they created. Far more memorable was the fact that the lone resident of the last house remained immovable – though quite safe – while the blaze went on in the adjoining buildings!

Graphic pictures of the night shoot, which look virtually indistinguishable from a real emergency.

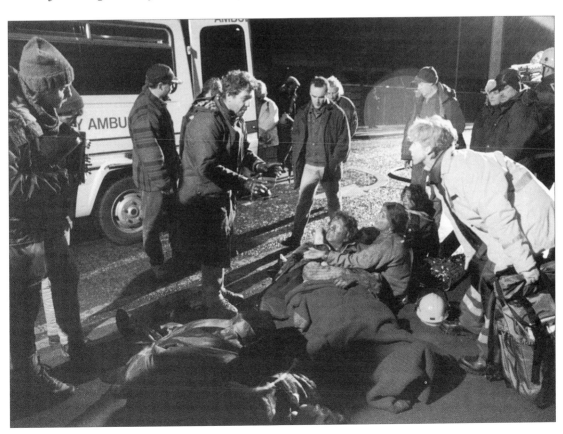

LIFE ON THE WARD

THE GENERAL MEDICAL WARD in Henry Park – which was formerly known as Ogden Ward and is to be found up on the second floor – comes to life on a working day almost as early as it would have done when Ancoats was a flourishing NHS hospital. Indeed at first glance very little seems to have changed – although now the patients in the beds are not ill but extras; the doctors and nursing staff are all actors; and, where one might expect to find an array of medical equipment ready for any emergency, instead there are all the trappings needed by a film crew.

Before seven o'clock in the morning, the building is opened up and the first grips, chargehands, joiners and dressers start arriving to begin their preliminary jobs for filming another half dozen or so scenes. Already, however, a lot of preparatory work has gone into making this day possible.

The cast and crew of 'Medics' normally work a five-day week from Sunday to Thursday – and on average put in a twelve-hour day to meet the exacting demands of the shooting schedule. A total of ten days is allowed for filming each episode, and two episodes are always shot back-to-back in a 'block' of twenty days.

The scripts for each episode have, ideally, been finalized by the script editors Bronagh Taggart and Philip Shelley some weeks earlier, although by the very nature of the series last-minute changes and rewrites are by no means unusual occurrences. An interesting colour scheme operates for these scripts, which enables anyone associated with the production to see at precisely what stage this fundamental working tool might be. White paper indicates a draft script, and blue the final. However, there is also a colour code for amendments which move dramatically through different shades of the rainbow as the deadline nears: pink, salmon, yellow and, finally, gold for any really last-minute change!

In a perfect world, producer Louise Berridge likes to have a script meeting to finalize the timing of the episode anything up to two weeks before the cast go into rehearsal. The actors then gather in Manchester three days before shooting and after a read-through start actual rehearsals while final preparations are made on the sets. Any locations required will almost certainly have been scouted earlier and the permission to use them cleared with the owners or the local authority.

One director is hired to make each

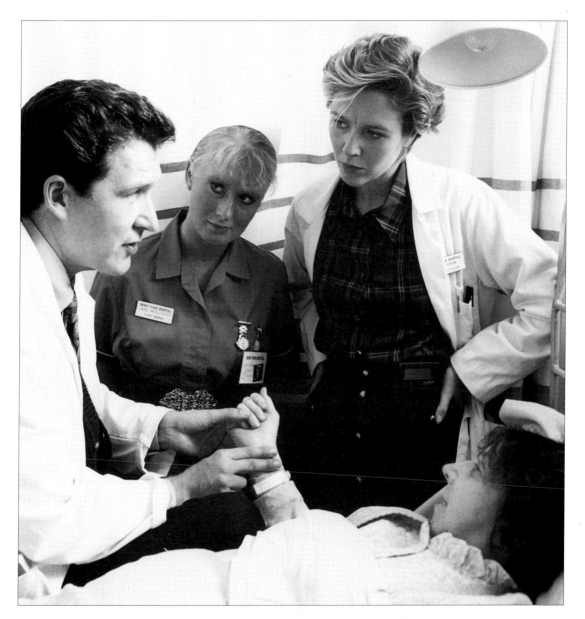

Just another day of demands on the skills of Dr Robert Nevin (James Gaddas) and Dr Gail Benson (Emma Cunningham) on the Henry Park wards.

pair of episodes and may well try and overlap with his predecessor for the sake of continuity – although this is naturally governed by their other commitments. Apart from meeting the regular members of the cast beforehand, each director normally gets together with any guest stars on the series a night or two before they are due to begin filming in order to discuss their particular roles.

Three of the key people behind the

complex operation that it takes to film 'Medics' are first assistant directors Ian Galley and John Friend Newman; second assistant director, Claire McCourt; and production co-ordinator Lynnette Carroll. Ian (or John) is the man on the set smoothing the director's path. Claire runs the production office in what were the old nurse's quarters in Ancoats, arranging everything from transport for the actors to hiring special props such as a laparoscope for a keyhole surgery scene. And Lynnette works out of Granada's headquarters in Quay Street keeping an eye on everything from the printing of scripts to the liaison between the producer and the rest of the unit.

Although the people called in for filming in the general medical ward can and do change regularly – in particular the guest actors and constant flow of extras – each day follows a fairly typical pattern. It is only the stories that are different.

My own visit coincided with the making of the fourth episode of the fifth series – a story which features a burns victim, a disillusioned clergyman who has discovered he has terminal cancer and a compulsive gambler – all mixed in with the emotional and practical dilemmas that beset the staff of Henry Park. The director for the episode was Tony Garner, an astute, quietly-spoken film-maker of wide experience whose most recent assignments have included two seasons on 'Soldier, Soldier' plus several episodes of that other well-known medical series, 'Peak Practice'.

Tony is a great believer in continu-ity, a fact which is very evident in his work. 'I believe it is important to perse-vere with any series that has something to say and entertains. You have to build on an audience by trying to introduce that extra something which will bring in more viewers. That's what we are attempting to do in this new series of "Medics".'

On any typical day's filming in the general ward it is more than likely that most, if not all, of the current five regu-lar members of the staff will be present – featuring as they do in all the stories: Dr Robert Nevin, the senior registrar; Dr Gail Benson, the senior house officer; registrar Dr Jay Rahman; charge nurse Billy Cheshire and Janice Thornton, the health care assistant. And in between watching them at work, it is interesting to discover how each has developed his or her character – all of whom have become increasingly familiar to viewers and made the ward in which they func-tion a familiar place with which any viewer who has ever been in hospital can identify.

Probably the most familiar of this group is James Gaddas, who has been playing the handsome, troubled Dr Nevin since the second series of 'Medics' and was recently dubbed by the *Daily Express* as 'the viewer's hearthrob'. James, who is over six foot tall, and has dark hair and a ready smile, is, however, the first to admit that taking on the role was not an easy decision. The reason being that he faints at the sight of blood and hates pain in any form.

'Of course, the blood we use on the

set is fake and I'm used to it by now,' he explains with a grin, 'but I do literally keel over at the sight of the real thing. I still get the wobblies when I see the heart machines and stuff in intensive care when we film there – because I know they are real and they've been used on real patients.'

Despite his squeamishness, James has made the role a key one in the series which he finds is a nice change from much of his earlier work on stage and TV where he was regularly cast in the role of villain! Born in Stockton-on-Tees, his father was a professional wrestler who fought under the name of 'Earl Warwick', but there was no theatrical precedent in the family when he decided to sign up for drama school at the age of eighteen.

'My dad taught me a few basic falls when I was young,' James recalls. 'He told me he knew what the acting business could be like and if ever I couldn't get any acting roles, I could at least take part in a couple of wrestling bouts to help pay the rent. Luckily it never happened – I would have been terrible if it had!'

After completing his training as an actor, he got his first job, appearing in *King Lear* at The Royal Exchange Theatre in Manchester.

'I had heard that carrying spears was the lot of new actors,' he says, with another ready smile. 'They must have thought I was pretty good because they gave me *six* to carry.'

Life on the stage was not one triumph after another, however, and James is still understandably grateful to his father for being so supportive.

'I remember one occasion when I wanted to take up an opportunity in Bristol. I was working in a butcher's shop and a men's outfitters during the day and as a barman at night, but I still couldn't raise enough money to get there. But then my father said to me, "I'll not have you full of regrets and looking over your shoulder for the rest of your life." And he handed over a bundle of notes saying, "That's to pay for your fare and digs".'

Subsequently, James Gaddas has played a variety of classical roles on the stage for the RSC and has appeared in a number of TV series including 'Dempsey & Makepeace', 'The Bill', 'Coronation Street' and 'The Camomile Lawn'. He also has a talent for stand-up comedy and as a member of the double act, The Sean Connery Brotherhood, has appeared regularly at the Comedy Store in London a very convenient location, since his home is in Muswell Hill.

After the succession of bad guys, James found Dr Nevin a really welcome break from type. 'I was absolutely hopeless at biology at school,' he confesses. 'But to research my role I did trail a doctor for several weeks to learn all about what they do. Although there is always an adviser on hand to make up for my lack of medical training, I do think I've picked up some know-how along the way – especially thanks to some of the real hospitals in which we've filmed.'

James particularly remembers the fourth series when the death of his lover

Dr Claire Armstrong made Dr Niven behave irrationally and unprofessionally and treat a young patient named Julie (played by Judy Brooke), who was suffering from pneumonia and severe jaundice, in a very cold and callous way.

'Dr Nevin behaved really badly then,' he recalls, 'making the patient feel she wasn't worth touching, let alone treating. But it goes to show that doctors are human and can get emotionally upset just the same as the rest of us.'

One sequence of this episode sticks in his mind for the embarrassment it caused him. 'The medical emergency happened when Julie's throat started bleeding profusely as a result of Hepatitis B and I had to try and stop it. I had to use a special instrument, push it down Julie's throat, inflate it and then shout, "Clamp" and "Unclamp" to those helping me. It's a complicated procedure and a real doctor has seven years to learn the technique. I had just fifteen minutes!

'The programme's medical adviser briefed me beforehand, of course, and then when the director called "Action!" I set to with enthusiasm. It was very messy with stage blood everywhere. When the director called "Cut!" I thought we'd completed the scene in one take. "Well done!" I was told. "That was splendid. Now we'll shoot it once more and let's see if this time you can put the tube at least into Julie's mouth rather than draping it across the bed." Was my face red!'

A rather more serious real-life drama occurred during filming that same

series. For while James was ostensibly resuscitating a heart victim for a scene in Henry Park, he heard that his father had suffered an actual heart attack and had been rushed to Teeside Hospital for emergency treatment.

'When I heard of his attack I was faced with a real dilemma,' he says, 'whether to go straight to the hospital or finish filming the scene. It sounds terribly mercenary to say it, but I stayed. I couldn't let everyone down and I knew Dad was in a comfortable condition. Granada had a car waiting to rush me over to see him as soon as the filming was over.'

Although Gaddas senior made a swift recovery, the worry was not quite over for James. His father told him that he was the latest in several generations of the family to have been afflicted by coronary problems and he wanted his son to take some tests.

'I did it to please him, and was very relieved to find out that everything was all right,' he says.

Dr Nevin is also about to try and put his own life right in 'Medics.'

'Although Robert is a good doctor, he has all these problems in his private life,' says James. 'And because he wants to be a consultant and these things matter they are holding him back. They say that consultancies are more about gravitas than actual ability and that is what he

Another member of the Henry Park team, Paramedic Penny Milner (Rosie Cavaliero) falling for the charms of Dr Nevin (James Gaddas) in series five.

is finding out. The result is that he's now trying to get control of his life. He's given up smoking, hardly drinks, plays squash and wants to sort out his love life. He's also about to take another job in the hospital.'

Louise Berridge reveals that this move will take Dr Nevin into the intensive care unit. 'It is such a wonderful place for drama,' she explains, 'because patients come into ITU from all over the hospital. You can have them of all ages and with all sorts of different ailments. There is also something about ITU – it is a kind of twilight zone, it's dark, and produces a very intense emotional bonding between patients and doctors. For Robert it also represents a good stepping stone from senior registrar to consultant and that's where he's going to be putting his energies.'

When he is not filming, James Gaddas is a keen motorcyclist 'a bike helps me to avoid the terrible traffic jams in London and reminds me that I'm still fairly young!' – and enjoys prowling around antique shops. He is also pursuing a career as a scriptwriter: his stage play, *Dream Rider*, has been filmed with Harold Hopkins and James Blundell, while another play, *Shadow Boxing*, inspired by the champion boxer, Chris Eubank, recently opened in Australia starring David Field from the TV soap, 'Home and Away'.

But much as James enjoys the role of Dr Nevin he is always nervous of approaches from fans. 'I love acting,' he smiles, 'but if anyone mistook me for a real doctor, I'd put them right sharpish.

A little knowledge can be a dangerous thing!'

If James Gaddas is the 'heartthrob' of 'Medics', then Emma Cunningham who plays Dr Gail Benson – and with whom Dr Nevin has already had a torrid love affair – is the 'sex symbol'. Certainly that is how a double-page spread in the *Daily Mirror* recently described the beautiful blonde senior house officer – although she herself insists she is 'not a sexy person and I don't dress provocatively'. In fact, although always immaculate on duty, when she is not filming Emma is happiest in jeans and a functional top.

There is no doubt, however, that she has won a large fan following playing Dr Benson, the efficient and ambitious doctor who seems to epitomize the successful career woman. Although she has had to temper her desire to move into surgery, Gail has more than once proved herself a brilliant diagnostician and capable manager of people.

Despite only being in her mid-twenties, Emma Cunningham has built her success as an actress on hard work and her achievements in 'Medics' on careful research. Born in Hayling Island, Hampshire, she says she was in love with acting from her childhood and first started to learn about drama at South Downs College from her lecturer, Rob Roberts. The next step was a course at the London Academy of Music and Dramatic Art – but she admits to having been apprehensive about leaving her parents' idyllic thatched cottage in Hampshire for life in the big city.

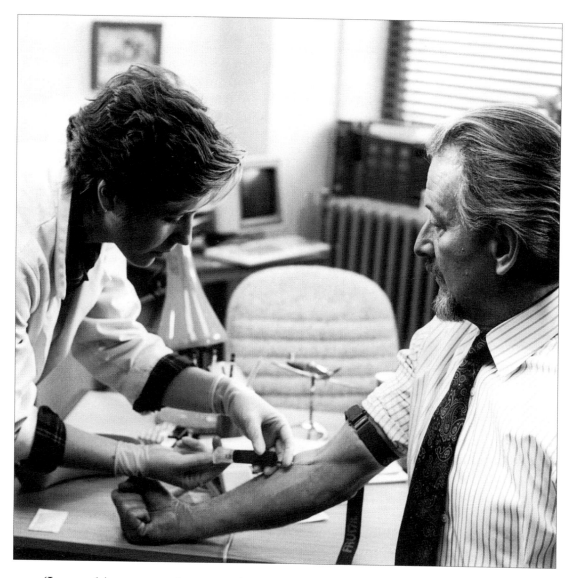

'I was a bit nervous about coming to the Big Smoke,' she confesses with one of her winning smiles. 'So I changed my image. I began developing a masculine, aggressive way of walking and talking. I could have bought a can of mace, but I thought a new appearance would be better. One experience I had made me even more determined. I was in a London tube station lift when I was touched up.

Dr Gail Benson (Emma Cunningham) doctoring one of her own colleagues, Senior Consultant Professor Douglas Beaumont (Ronald Pickup).

It was horrible. I couldn't tell who it had been. Then it happened again, so I let out a stream of four-letter words. I wasn't frightened, just offended, and I wanted this man to be shocked and embarrassed.'

After leaving LAMDA, Emma helped to set up a fringe theatre company, Arts Threshold, and the group's first production, *The Guise* by David Mowat, won the prestigeous 'Fringe First' award at the Edinburgh Festival. It also provided Emma with the chance to break into television.

She worked in another award-winning production (an Emmy this time) when she played Juliet in a BBC Shakespeare Workshop – before coming to widespread public attention in the series 'Minder', playing Ray Daley's girlfriend, Gloria. Prior to joining 'Medics' in the second series, Emma also appeared in two of the top TV cop series, 'Van Der Valk' and 'Inspector Morse'. Subsequently she has also appeared alongside Cherie Lunghi in the Kenco coffee TV commercial.

When she was offered the role in 'Medics', Emma says she immediately appreciated that realism was one of the keynotes to the series and flung herself into research.

'I was invited along to St Thomas's Hospital in London and spent some time as an observer in the casualty department,' she recalls. 'The patients had to be asked for their permission before I could look on. I saw some horrific injuries while I was there.

'There was one man who had stepped on to an open corned-beef can and almost sliced his heel off. As the doctor was pointing out the details of the injury to me I was nodding and staying calm when in fact I was horrified. But I couldn't show my true feelings because that would have upset the patient. It was great to be shown the ropes by real medical staff, and the experience convinced me I wouldn't run away from an emergency – I'd *do* something about it.'

Emma has brought much of this composure to her role in the four years she has been on the screen. Her earlier unpleasant experience also enabled her to show the right degree of gravitas when Dr Benson found herself the object of a stream of sexist and personal criticism while at work.

'I'm not the giggly female I used to be,' she admits. 'I specifically cultivated the way I am as protection. Surprising as it may seem I do occasionally get mistaken for a man when I'm striding about in my boots – or else because of my short, cropped hair. Recently I was collecting some airline tickets and a man shouted across the floor, "Can you get this young man his tickets?" I was with my boyfriend at the time, so I unzipped my jacket, stuck out my chest and said, "Young man?"'

There is, in fact, an interesting story behind this change of hairstyle from Emma's original long, flowing locks which all came about as a result of her role in 'Medics'. It was due to a case of mistaken identity.

'The "Medics" production department thought that in some shots – and

Opposite: A smile to brighten up any patient's day from Emma Cunningham as Dr Gail Benson, before the big haircut!

especially back-of-head shots – I bore too much of a resemblance to another of the doctors, Dr Alison Makin, who is played by Teddie Thompson. Viewers were apparently confusing us because of our long blonde hair and similar cheek-bone construction. Initially, they had Teddie dye her hair brown, but when this didn't work they asked if I'd have my hair cut to avoid the confusion.

'At first I wasn't happy, because I thought it was my greatest asset. But after I had spoken to several hairdressers for advice I was quite keen on the idea. And now that it's done I'm very happy – people take me more seriously – and it's so much easier to deal with. I wish I'd done it sooner!'

Change of image or not, Emma has still gathered a host of admirers – one of whom became such a nuisance last year that she had to consider changing the phone number of her flat in Fulham.

'I had this call from a guy who asked for me and then said how much he liked "Medics". I didn't think any more of it – until he turned up on my doorstep the next day. I was horrified and just spoke to him through the window while I pretended there was someone else with me.'

This, she says, is one of the prices to be paid for appearing in a popular TV series. But sometimes recognition can be of great assistance – as it was in the summer of 1994 when she was about to fly off on holiday from Gatwick to visit her Greek boyfriend. In fact, she sparked off a full-scale security alert.

'My boyfriend runs a diving and watersports school on the island of Spetses,' she says, 'and during my previous trip I had brought home some sophisticated electronic nautical equipment for repair. I was carrying the gear in several large bags, and because I enjoy producing small sculptures I also had a few sachets of modelling clay packed in as well.

'Unfortunately, on the airport X-ray machine, the diving equipment resembled bomb-making apparatus and the clay gave the impression of being Semtex high explosive! I was about to be taken away for questioning when one of the burly security guards said, "Hey – it's Gloria from 'Minder'!" It's the only time I've been recognized and extremely relieved about it.'

Emma was able to explain the unusual contents of her bags and still catch her flight to be with her boyfriend – whom she joins on the beautiful Greek island whenever her acting commitments permit. Although not a regular exerciser, she enjoys wind-surfing, water-skiing and swimming – all pursuits she can easily indulge in on Spetses.

'But appearing in "Medics" has made me wary about how long I spend in the Greek sun,' she says. 'I have fair skin and lots of moles so although I like to get a tan I do have regular check-ups.'

Emma has not only been made aware of the danger of cancer – but also the problems of ageing. She has, in fact, just taken out a pension funded by her TV work.

'Don't get me wrong, I feel very fit at the moment. But my character has to deal with a lot of old people and I've come to realize that, well, none of us are getting any younger. I don't want to turn round one day when I'm sixty and find that I haven't made any provision for my old age. Being old and not having enough money to get by on must be awful.'

Although Emma Cunningham is now one of the most familiar faces both on and off the 'Medics' set, she still laughs at one incident that took place early in her association with the series.

'It happened during my first series. We had just finished this take, and they were setting up the next shot, when a cameraman came in and said, "Right get rid of that blonde." I was fuming, and if I was slightly more of a prima donna, I would have said something. It was not until eighteen months later that I realized "blonde" is the name for a type of light used in filming. Can you imagine if I *had* said anything?'

Dr Jay Rahman, the house officer on the ward, who is played by Jimmi Harkishin, also has something of a reputation among viewers as a heart-throb and is currently Gail's love interest in the series. A brilliant and also passionately

Dr Jay Rahman (Jimmi Harkishin) using a little of his well-known charm on Dr Gail Benson (Emma Cunningham).

committed doctor, Jay is as good-looking as he is unconventional and can amuse people as easily as he can alarm them by his off-beat behaviour. Having said this, he is perhaps the best medic on the ward and particularly good at looking after chronically sick patients.

Because of his darkly handsome good looks, Jay also attracts more than professional attention from both female patients and colleagues, and was the object of infatuation for a student doctor during series four. In the new series, his relationship with Gail is under threat from a new character, the beautiful red-headed consultant, Dr Diana Hardy, who stirs more than an interest in research in him . . .

'Last year it was Dr Nevin's turn to have his oats,' Jimmi laughs, 'but now it is Jay's turn. The thing is, he's rather a reluctant sex god! In a way he is a bit like me. I am the reverse of the dumb blonde. People don't expect me to look like this and have a brain as well. I have worried about it quite a lot from time to time because I'm sick and tired of being cast in macho roles when what I want is to be deep. That's one of the reasons I like working in 'Medics' because playing Jay has given me a chance to create a character of real depth and personality.'

Jimmi's undeniable good looks are due in no small measure to his half-Italian, half-Indian background which has given him a natural aura of mystery. He was actually born in Paris, although he grew up in both Italy and India, and came to England when his father – a textile merchant in Bangalore – moved

here. He first got the urge to become an actor, he says, when he was studying at North London College. He was invited to appear in a new play, *A-Z*, which went on to win an Evening Standard Drama Award. He was just eighteen and had found his calling.

'I have to say I never wanted to be in the medical profession,' he admits, 'but I suspect my father would have been keen on the idea. Education was the be all and end all to him. He certainly didn't want me to be an actor. He would have much preferred me to be a businessman, a lawyer or a doctor. The thing is I can be all those things on the screen. I also wanted to party all night and have lots of pretty girls round me – honestly, that's one of the reasons I decided to become an actor!'

Like so many other young hopefuls, Jimmi did not find work easy to come by in his early days and apart from working as a barman and on a building site, he has also been a professional musician. But persistence paid off and apart from stage credits in *A View From The Bridge*, *Saved* and *Kiss of the Spiderwoman*, he has been seen on TV in 'Shalom, Shalom', 'Eurocops'; and notably as the feckless lawyer Krish in the BBC drama series, 'South Of The Border'.

Jimmi was immediately attracted to the role of Jay Rahman when it was offered to him for the second series because of his conviction that 'Medics'

Opposite: Brilliant doctor and ladies' man Dr Jay Rahman, played by Jimmi Harkishin.

was intended to be so different from all the other medical dramas. He had, in fact, a more intimate knowledge of the programme than all the other newcomers at that time for he had actually appeared briefly in the original series playing a student taking part in a rag-week stunt at Henry Park.

'The thing that is so good about "Medics" – unlike "Casualty" or "Cardiac Arrest" – is that it goes into the personal lives of the staff. It's like a soap with a heart – more like "St Elsewhere" or "LA Law".'

Jimmi's impact as Dr Rahman has brought him a large fan mail as well as a number of newspaper stories about his off-screen romances. As a result he has given some thought to the way he is perceived by both the public and the press.

'I suppose you become a composite image for some people,' he explains. 'Doctors are supposed to be caring and when you are ill they knock you out and do things to you – that's a powerful combination. They appear to be glamorous, when in reality most of them are overworked and underpaid and not at all like they appear on screen.'

He has also built up a background for his character Jay Rahman to help him play the registrar with greater conviction.

'I decided that he probably came from working-class stock and then went to a grammar school. Like a lot of second generation Asians, he has this parental pressure on him not to fail. So while a lot of his peers are probably crack dealers or window cleaners – with the odd accountant among them – he went into medicine. And the boy has done good!'

The actor himself has also 'done good' to the extent that he is able to indulge what he calls his 'decadent tastes' for travel, designer suits, powerful motor bikes and bungee jumping. The exposure that 'Medics' has given his distinctive looks also means that he does not go unnoticed in the street.

'People do seem to recognize me now,' he says with a wry smile. 'But it can be very strange at times. I live in Haringey and one guy was looking at me in the street there recently and he was obviously very disappointed. He probably thought I should be there in my white coat and stethoscope, just as he sees me in 'Medics'.

'I don't usually tell people that I'm an actor when I meet them for the first time – especially when I am away from this country. That's one of the great things about having a bit of money to spend, it means I can travel to places such as the USA where I spent two months last year. I get paid an awful lot for not doing very much, but I suppose real success is knowing how to spend it. I've got the freedom to take on different kinds of work as well – and to turn things down. I do television for my wallet, but it is nice to be able to afford to do stage work, too, for the soul.'

Despite his high profile in 'Medics', Jimmi does not believe he will become typecast. 'I don't think so, because in the theatre I seem to keep getting cast as blond Italians which means I have to dye my hair. I look so different I defy anyone who watches 'Medics' to recognize me!'

The remaining two members of the staff of the general ward are the hard-worked charge nurse Billy Cheshire, played by Clarence Smith, and the irrepressible health care assistant, Janice Thornton (Susan McCardle). Although Billy became popular with viewers during the fourth series, Janice is one of the bright new characters making her debut in the latest series of episodes.

According to the production team, Billy was deliberately introduced into 'Medics' to try and strike a balance in a cast that was wholly doctors and patients. It was also important to ensure that viewers did not get the impression that it is doctors alone who work inordinate hours caring for patients – whereas, in fact, as much as ninety per cent of the day-to-day care is being administered by the nursing staff. Billy is seen as representing the role of nursing in the ward – and has provided a challenging and constantly evolving role for Clarence Smith.

'There is always a danger that a hospital series can get a bit too doctor-orientated,' says Clarence, 'and Billy is there to underline that "Medics" is about everyone in Henry Park from the top administrators through the surgical and doctoring staff to those of us on the ward floor. And believe you me, the hours that guys like Billy and assistants like Janice work can even put some of the doctors in the shade!'

Londoner Clarence, a quick-witted young actor with a marvellous sense of humour, came to 'Medics' after a varied career. Apart from classical roles at the Royal Shakespeare Company, he has appeared in contemporary productions such as *Blood Brothers, Charity Event* and *Our Country's Good* at the Royal Court Theatre. He was also co-founder of the Double Edge Theatre and has written/directed *The Remnant* and *Johnny Was A Good Man*. As well as a couple of film roles in 'Half Moon Street' and 'Ford On Waters', he has appeared on television in 'The Bill', 'Full Stretch' and 'Casualty'.

To research for his role in 'Medics', Clarence spent two weeks trailing a charge nurse in Finchley Hospital, London. 'I realized then what caring and professional people they are – and also how much they see of the strains and tensions between doctors. The charge nurse really has to be on the ball when the men and women in the white coats are under pressure. He's got to mediate between them and the patients, especially when the patients – who are naturally worried themselves – also get worked up and irrational.

'Charge Nurses like Billy are always trying to tell the administrators that the wards are understaffed; that the standard of care is under threat because they are being constantly asked to save money by closing wards or moving staff around. Billy believes in hands-on nursing and is constantly worried that this is in danger of being replaced by technology. He has to have all his training and his wits about him the whole time.'

Clarence has created a very believable figure in Billy – so believable, in fact, that once while filming at Tameside

he was stopped by a real patient.

'She asked me which way to go to find a particular ward,' he smiles. 'I looked at her and said, "I'm sorry – I'm not real." But as she walked away I got the impression she was not altogether convinced!'

When out of his blue, high-necked uniform Billy has also been asked more than once by people what kind of role he is playing in 'Medics'. 'I tell them I'm a charge nurse – the caring face of the National Health. The immediate response is, "Pull the other one"!'

The dedicated charge nurse, Billy Cheshire, around whom much of the activity of the ward flows, played by Clarence Smith.

Amusing as many of the incidents which Clarence has experienced since joining 'Medics' undoubtedly are – the other side of the coin has involved him in no fewer than three accidents.

'I'm not normally accident-prone,' he protests, 'but look what's happened to me since I started filming the series? I've been knocked off my bike by a police car and on another occasion had my glasses broken while travelling to work. Then in the early hours of one morning my BMW was hit by a couple of kids joy-riding in a stolen car. My mate and I drove after them until they finally crashed the vehicle. We both jumped out and managed to catch one. That all happened about five hours before I was due to start filming!'

The fifth series will lift the lid on Billy's life outside the hospital. As producer Louise Berridge explains: 'We think this aspect about him has been very neglected. In that uniform he looks almost like a Russian commissar and can appear very humourless and forbidding – which, of course, he isn't. We know that he has a wife and children and we want to explore that and how it affects his life in the hospital and his relationship with patients – female in particular.'

The relationship between Billy and Janice Thornton is also being developed in the fifth series. Initially, the pair are at loggerheads as the young health care assistant seems to make one mistake after another, either in her ward duties or when dealing with patients.

'But it's hardly surprising she gets things wrong when you realize she's been thrown in the deep end with hardly any specialized training,' says petite, bubbly Susan McArdle. 'But she cares about the patients so much and can't bear to see them suffer. To begin with she finds it very difficult to refuse any request and that gets her into trouble with Billy. They get off on the wrong foot, but gradually things improve as he realizes she is a hard worker and her heart is in the right place.'

The introduction of health care assistants is one of the new moves by the NHS which is intended to take some of the more manual tasks away from the nursing staff so that they can concentrate on caring for patients – and an element that 'Medics' wants to reflect. 'They are there to do all sorts of things,' says Susan, 'serve meals, fetch this and that, give and take, even chat to patients. All the simple little things which are still an important part of the medical service.'

Susan, who is just over five foot tall, with dazzling blue-green eyes and dark hair, was born in Manchester and though she had several accidents as a child says she was taken to just about every other hospital in the city except Ancoats. Determined that acting was to be her career, she trained at the Italia Conti Academy, where her tiny figure ideally suited her for teenage roles. Her early work consisted of stage productions of *The Prince and the Pauper, Aspects of Dance* and *The Wizard of Oz*, before her appearances at the Oldham Coliseum as Cherry in *Sinbad the Sailor* and Mary McGinty in *Once A Catholic*. Prior to joining the cast of 'Medics' she was cast as Siobhan in the BBC's 'Once Upon A Time In The North' which starred Bernard Hill.

'Before I started filming I spent sev- eral days watching auxiliaries at work in a local hospital,' she recalls. 'They get about four days' basic training and then suddenly find themselves in the midst of everything in a frantically busy general ward. My life acting what they do in real- ity is an absolute doddle by comparison.'

Susan has every intention of staying with the series as long as she is asked. 'Janice is a lovely char- acter,' she says, 'and she intends to make a go of her life. She is going to start taking her NVQs and is deter- mined to become a qualified nurse. There is also a possible rela- tionship with Billy – which won't be sexual although there will be hints. But I'm afraid I can't say any more about that at the moment!'

Susan McArdle plays Janice Thornton, the bubbly new health care assistant finding her way in the fifth series.

The Blood and Gore Team

One of the most realistic features of 'Medics' has been the make-up of patients suffering from all manner of illnesses as well as many different kinds of injury and burns. The backroom team responsible for the series' blood and gore is lead by make-up supervisors Linda Strath and Margaret O'Keefe, augmented by nursing adviser, Dympna Donegan, plus Simon Tytherleigh, a specialist in medical make-up.

Linda and Margaret both use detailed photographs of actual patients and accident victims for guidance – and the gallery of these shots which hang in the make-up department in the old nurses quarters of Ancoats are enough to turn a delicate stomach over first thing in the morning! For the two ladies, though, it represents quite a change from the normal make-up required in TV drama series and a personal challenge to ensure that every medical detail is accurate. With this objective in mind it is nothing unusual to find either one busy singeing a wig to simulate burned hair; preparing vivid red scars and cuts to be stuck on as body injuries; or streaking an actor with blood and sticking the most horrendous cuts and bruises over the rest of his face. Undoubtedly the most grisly task undertaken by the team was creating a shattered knee – the actor in question having to conceal the lower half of his leg in the ground before the accident scene could be shot.

Dympna Donegan, who is a senior nursing sister working in Manchester, brings a lifetime of experience of real injuries to her role as adviser. Apart from giving advice about the latest practices in curative medicine, she also passes judgement on the authenticity of cuts and burns, and can explain to members of the cast what any particular injury feels like to the sufferer and how the pain should be portrayed on the screen.

Simon Tytherleigh, who has a reputation as one of the best specialists in his field, delights in what he calls his 'grotesque works of art'. The basis of this art is gellatine applied to the skin and then painted, sprayed and powdered to create the effect of a specific injury. He often uses plastic 'bald caps' to cover a performer's own hair in order to create head wounds and the loss of hair from fire accidents. Among his creations have been false torsos for operation sequences; the body of a crushed child; and the tiny figure of a new-born baby made from gellatine in which he inserted a small bladder to simulate breathing.

Perhaps the oddest request to the 'Medics' make-up team came during the fourth episode of the latest series. They were asked to make up a burns victim who, in despair, had hanged herself. However, only her legs were to be seen dangling in the shot – and although one of the most regularly used techniques for this kind of TV 'suicide' is to sit the 'corpse' on a beam, director Tony Garner insisted on 'authenticity'. And

that was how a local extra earned her fee
by spending the day suspended in a body
harness from the ceiling of a linen room
outside the burns unit in Ancoats!

*A striking example of the make-up artist's skill,
as seen in an episode from the fourth series.*

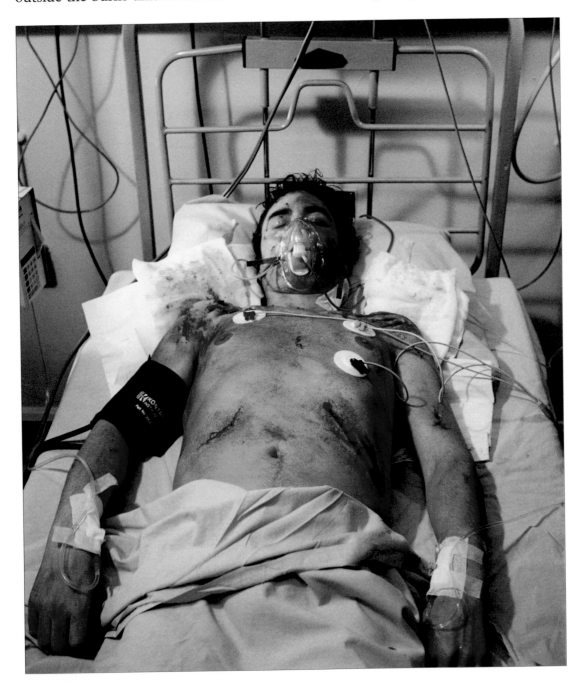

THE DOCTOR WHO HAS RETURNED

THE CIRCLE of dish-shaped theatre lights are already throwing a stark white illumination across the green operating table in the centre of the room. Around it stand trolleys of equipment ready with all the gleaming silver knives, scalpels and clamps required by a surgeon and his assistants for their delicate operations. And at the head of the table, a bank of high-tech machines to measure everything from a patient's blood count to his heart beat similarly await the arrival of the surgical team.

Less obtrusive lights are also on in the adjoining scrub room where the team will prepare for their day's work; while adjoining this facility is a second operating theatre: at present not required, but showing every sign that it could be swung into action at a moment's notice. There is also a kind of tension in the air which is said to be unique to operating theatres . . . although this theatre is actually quite unlike any other to be found at any hospital in the British Isles.

For the 'operating theatre suite' – as it is officially designated – is an optical illusion. Situated on the second floor of Ancoats Hospital, it is only real in the sense of having once been the hospital's surgical heart, but is now the exclusive domain of the film crew involved in shooting 'Medics'.

Unlike any of the other areas of Ancoats which have been adapted to the needs of film-making, the operating suite is still much as it was when the last surgeon and his team left almost two years ago. But whereas the other wards and offices in the building have required redesigning and refurbishing by Granada's backroom boys, the sheer size of this place provides the technicians with enough room to bring in comfortably all the cameras, sound equipment and extra pieces of lighting that will enable viewers to be eye-witnesses to the very heart of a hospital's daily work.

The tension, though, is unmistakably genuine – for the crew have set up the theatre to film an operation and the star performer is now awaited. When he arrives, everyone is instantly aware that they are in the presence of one of the genuine eccentrics of TV and a man who has become something of a legend thanks to portraying a traveller in time who used to hop around the galaxies in an old-fashioned blue police box called a Tardis.

'How's Tom this morning?' a sound technician enquires of a passing grip.

'He's on his way from make-up,' the man replies. 'He's bubbling. Three minutes and he'll be here.'

The words are spoken with a mixture of anticipation and excitement. They are quite evidently based on many months of working with the man who has now created a second memorable doctor character for the small screen – Tom Baker, the former fourth and arguably most popular Doctor Who, and now Professor Geoffrey Hoyt, Henry Park's formidable consultant surgeon.

The adrenalin level rises as the countdown continues. Then, as suddenly and dramatically as he used to appear as the Time Lord from Gallifrey, Tom Baker is on the set and his vibrant personality seems to fill the entire suite.

'How *are* we all this morning?' he booms as he strides through the assembly of crew members. The mass of curly brown locks which he once attempted to restrain under a trilby hat have now gone, to be replaced by neatly-parted, short grey hair; and the swirling coat and 23-foot long, multicoloured scarf have given way to the green gown and face mask of a surgeon. But the large, protruding blue eyes, mouth full of glistening teeth and the sense of bonhomie which hangs around him like an aura are still very much there. The face may be a

Tom Baker delights in entertaining the cast and crew of 'Medics', both in front of the camera and behind it during a break in filming.

little fleshier now, but the confrontational stare is still the same. This is the man whose adventures with aliens and monsters once used to frighten childen behind their chairs, but now terrorizes the staff of Henry Park to the delight of a new, if somewhat older, audience.

Tom's eyes roam around the set and he is instantly aware of the presence of a stranger. Me.

'Who are you?' he enquires in a voice that mixes a sense of fun with not-altogether-serious intimidation. He actually knows very well – but on occasions like this he cannot resist playing to the gallery. I explain I'm here to watch the filming and the grin becomes even wider.

'Ah, so you've come to watch a benevolent tyrant at work,' he says, ever the master of the instant quote. 'I suppose you could call me the James Robertson Justice of the 1990s.' (James Robertson Justice (1905-1975) was the imposing actor with a booming voice and luxuriant red beard who is best remembered for his role as the irascible surgeon Sir Launcelot Spratt in the hugely successful British comedy film, *Doctor in the House* (1954) and its several sequals.)

Almost immediately, Tom turns away to talk about the day's filming with director Tony Garner. As always he has come prepared with some ideas of his own which he wants to discuss. Though ready to argue a point, he is never averse to accepting another view and invariably listens to the opinions of his fellow performers. There is no doubting that he is a thoroughgoing professional – but one whose sense of the absurd and love of eccentricity is never far from the surface of his personality.

To those who know something of medical history in Manchester there is something almost eerie about the manner in which Tom Baker is playing Geoffrey Hoyt. For there are very strong echoes in his performance of a man named Sir Geoffrey Jefferson (1886-1961) who is remembered in Ancoats as one of the doyens of neurosurgery and a man 'with one of the most searching and original minds in British surgery,' to quote some biographical notes written about him.

Born the son of a GP in Rochdale, Jefferson graduated in Manchester in 1909 and five years later won the gold medal in the master of surgery examination. His later achievements as a neurosurgeon lead to his knighthood in 1950, at the same time as his forceful personality and unique style of operating made him a truly awesome figure in local medical circles. His philosophy, based on his years of working on the human brain, was easily summarized. Clinical study was the sheet anchor of patient care and 'gadgets' must be kept in their place.

In his performance as Professor Hoyt, Tom Baker has also created a man whose intuition and hands-on experience, not forgetting his genuine concern for patients, has shown him to be a unique, if somewhat eccentric, medic. And like James Robertson Justice's Spratt, to whom he has already been compared, Hoyt is a man whose bark is frequently worse than his bite.

The fifth series of 'Medics' has, interestingly, given Hoyt a clearer chance to explain his own reasons for becoming a doctor and what drives him on. In a revealing scene in episode four (written by Paul Abbott) he is seen talking to an

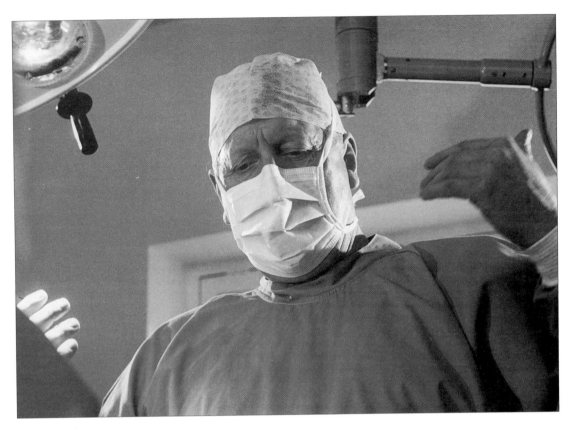

old friend and unburdening himself in a rare moment of confession.

'I have very clear memories about why I chose medicine,' he says. 'It was transparent to everyone else that I'd have made a better lawyer than a doctor, but I believed . . . I truly believe in the NHS – greatest good for the greatest number. Nye Bevan and the big parade. And after forty years, I watch these individuals come in and turn it into a lottery. Greatest good for the smallest numbers. Mmn? Cynical business school medicine. Tampering with my religion till I wonder what the big parade was all about. It's made me cynical . . .'

In the scene about to be filmed (from episode three, written by Neil McKay), Tom is going to reveal the other side of his character – the joker behind the gauze mask.

Hoyt is completing surgery on a patient while being watched at work by a group of students. He is in a good mood – matching that of the star himself – and the feeling is intensified by a background track of classical music of the kind which is now commonplace in modern operating theatres. As Tom waits for the final adjustments to camera, sound and lighting, he continues to amuse the company with anecdotes about other actors he has worked with – 'Nicol Williamson, one of our greatest actors: now there was a man who created an aura around him' – insights into his current reading – 'Julian Barnes' *Letters From London*, quite brilliant' – and then a humorous exchange

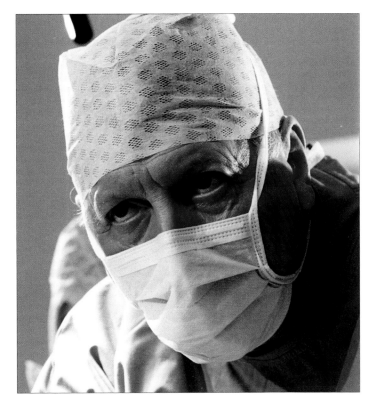

Professor Geoffrey Hoyt is one of the most brilliant surgeons in his field and with expert advice and a close atention to detail, Tom Baker has made his character a totally believable figure.

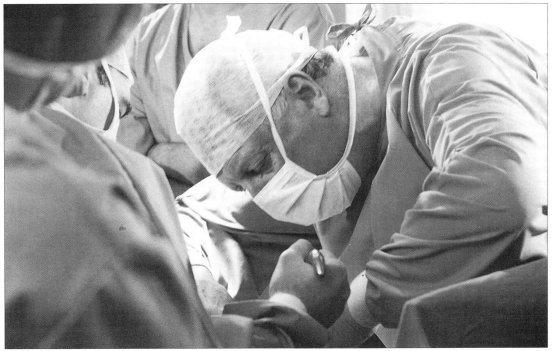

with one of the other actors who is clearly rehearsing not only some of his own lines, but the replies of Baker himself.

'You obviously know the whole script?' Tom grins.

'Well, I have read it all.'

'That's cheating!' is the immediate response.

Tom begins to pace about again, head sunk on to his chest, seemingly concentrating on his own performance. He passes me and stops once more. 'If you want a sentence to summarize my career in medicine then how about this: "He has gone from a bottom-wiper to a surgeon in one fell swoop!"'

Grinning wickedly, he walks away without a backward glance and I know I shall have to wait until we talk later to appreciate the full significance of the remark.

Tony Garner calls for action and Tom slips effortlessly into the role of the surgeon. Four years in the part have certainly provided him with a practised skill that is impossible not to admire.

On the operating table, a fake torso from the neck to the lower abdomen has been carefully positioned so that the deception is not visible to the camera. Tom bends over this, waits for his cue, and then speaks to the little knot of students – all extras who are gathered around him.

'And this is a cholecystecomy,' he booms. 'A pretty routine operation, but you'll all have noticed I've made a complete hash of it. Can anyone tell me why?'

The piercing blue eyes circle the students, none of whom seems to have the nerve to answer.

'Because I need the poor lady back next month to boost our intake figures. We must all keep striving to keep the surgical director happy!'

A laugh breaks the silence as Hoyt turns his attention back to the table and, indicating the 'body' in front of him, orders: 'Close her up!'

Tony Garner calls 'cut' and goes into an immediate huddle with Tom Baker. He is obviously not completely happy and a second take is set up. Tom eases off his mask by untying one of the strings as they talk and the action suddenly reminds me of an earlier piece of surgery he had filmed for episode one (written by Robin Mukherjee). He was also instructing a group of students then and had asked one to identify a piece of anatomy. When the girl was unable to answer, he had replied: 'It's the bile duct, for goodness' sake. What else could it be? His *lunch*?'

Later in that same scene he had delivered another typical riposte of the kind that has made his appearances in the series so popular.

'Of course, only one other profession resembles surgery in almost every respect,' he whispered. 'Robbery. We mask up for the job. Wear gloves. We dig for our loot and if the job goes wrong, regretfully, we bury it. Cut please!'

A moment after the memory of these words had gone through my mind, Tom Baker was repeating the scene and this time everyone was satisfied . . .

The Tom Baker who strides into the actor's green room half an hour later to talk about his role as Hoyt is a quite different man. An open-necked shirt and fawn overcoat have replaced the surgeon's gown while in his hand he is cradling a cup of coffee instead of a scalpel.

Although Tom has a natural scepticism about journalists – too many reporters have tried to pry into his chequered public and private life in the past – and he certainly does enjoy making grandiloquent gestures and offering provocative comments. When one has talked to him for any length of time he emerges as a man who revels in his profession, although he too often disguises his achievements behind deliberately outrageous remarks.

His career before 'Medics' makes for interesting – and relevant – reading. He was born in Liverpool just over sixty years ago, where his mother was a cleaner and his father a sailor.

'At first I was ashamed of my parents,' he says. 'The house was dirty because my mother was out cleaning other people's homes. Now I'm ashamed of that attitude. She loved me unconditionally, but gave me rather upsetting advice, "Tell the truth, keep your bowels open, say your prayers, know your place and always polish your shoes." My parents also didn't speak to each other for nine years. I remember the melodrama which I liked.

'But right from being a child I wanted to be a star,' he goes on, the smile growing larger on his face, 'not just an actor, so I thought I'd start by becoming a saint. I was deeply religious, you see, so at fifteen I became the first member of my family to leave Liverpool and went to Jersey and entered a monastery belonging to the brothers of the Order of Ploermel. I stayed there for six years, but ended up a martyr to my lust. I was besotted with my fellow celibates, but there was no chance to score. I enjoyed the suffering and deprivation and silence, although I haven't stopped talking since!'

Tom pauses and swigs another mouthful of coffee. Time may have extenuated the circumstances of some of these events, but they are nonetheless interesting to listen to.

'After I left the monastery I did my national service, which actually gave me my first taste of hospital life. I was in the Medical Corps in Germany and got my first experience of handling corpses. In fact I got to feel quite comfortable in hospital. Following national service I spent some time as a medical orderly on board the Queen Mary which sailed to any number of exciting places. The result was that I'm not frightened about moping up blood or even wiping patients' backsides!'

A huge roar of laughter burst from Tom and he looked closely at me for a response. The relevance of his earlier remark on the set was now apparent.

'I have often thought since then that I would have made a rather good doctor,' he goes on. 'I think I'd be quite an expert at putting patients' minds at rest. After all, at moments like those doctors are doing nothing more than putting on performances.'

In fact what Tom *did* do after his time at sea was to go to drama school. After training, he worked with various repertory companies before gaining a contract with the National Theatre and played a variety of roles including the Prince of Morocco in Laurence Olivier's much-praised production of *The Merchant of Venice*. After that he started breaking into films, most notably as Rasputin in *Nicholas and Alexandra* and then television.

It was in 1974 that he was offered the role of the fourth Doctor Who – and his life has never been the same again. Almost singlehanded he turned the BBC series into an international success and became a household name as well as the focus of a cult following that has never diminished since he gave up the part in 1982. To many people he remains the best of all the Doctors and he never minds in the slightest being linked to the role.

'It was the happiest job and the biggest success I have ever had,' (a twinkle sparkles in his eyes). 'It was a marvellous part and I got hold of it and the children liked what I did. Nowadays I even meet producers who grew up watching it!

'I've heard that some actors don't like talking about their past roles. I really don't understand that – because we are the products of our past. If you are a public performer you are inextricably linked with what you have appeared in. When Geoff Hurst is in a pub I don't suppose he gets tired of people saying, "That's Geoff Hurst – he scored a hat-trick in a world cup final"! I was a children's hero for six years and no one will ever be able to take that away from me. And the evidence is still there on film and is being shown all over the world.'

Tom, in fact, is frequently invited to places such as America to address Doctor Who fans about his years in the role and says he could actually make a living out of attending these conventions. 'Do you realize this tape we are making could be sold for $25 to the Doctor Who Society in America?'

In the same mockingly outrageous

Opposite: Tom Baker's sense of fun is occasionally allowed to creep into the personality of Professor Hoyt.

tones Tom says that he was a 'madman' to have given up the role.

'I got proprietorial and became demanding and insecure,' he recalls. 'I never meant to be difficult, but I began to live in the world of the Doctor, this benevolent alien, and thought no one understood me and I'd had enough. But of course I hand't. I could have gone on for ever. I've never really recovered.'

Truth to tell, Tom has recovered enough to make many more television appearances including Sherlock Holmes in 'The Hound of the Baskervilles', and a renegade priest (shades of his youth) in 'The Life and Loves of a She Devil'; not to mention stage appearances as Judge Brack in *Hedda Gabler*, Oscar Wilde in *Feasting With Panthers* and a wonderful Long John Silver in one of the Mermaid Theatre's productions of *Treasure Island*. He also got a lot of pleasure in presenting Yorkshire Television's 'The Book Tower' and doing a whole series of instantly recognizeable voice-overs for TV commercials.

It is, though, undoubtedly the role of Professor Geoffrey Hoyt that has brought him back to public notice and initiated a second stage of popular recognition. When he first began work on the series in Manchester, however, the fame of Doctor Who at once caught up with him again.

'I kept getting approached by these young people who got very emotional and disturbed when they recognized me. They would say things like, "We don't

want any money, Doctor – can't you just take us away with you in the Tardis and get us out of all this mess?" Seeing me, they remembered when they were ten, when they were happy and full of fun and sitting and watching "Doctor Who". Now fifteen years on they are in a mess and they have no jobs and they see no hope. Just like a real doctor I was being confronted by needy, suffering people who wanted something. But it was something I couldn't properly define, let alone give to them.'

Such encounters, however, helped him to develop the character of Hoyt whom he now sees as an eccentric in the same mould as Doctor Who – 'a man who allows actors like me to get up to all sorts of wonderful antics.' Newspaper critics have been quick to draw similar comparisons – Corinna Honan in the *Daily Mail*, spoke for many of her colleagues when she wrote in March 1992: 'No television role, with the arguable exception of Doctor Who, has ever tapped Baker's talents better. His commanding manner and relish for the macabre have proved well-suited to a larger-than-life consultant who flirts over post-mortems and cracks questionable jokes at the operating table.'

Although Tom did not deliberately study a specific surgeon on whom to model Geoffrey Hoyt, he has met several consultants and 'synthesized' the professor from various stories he was told about great physicians. 'They did seem to be a bunch of show-offs so that was the main basis,' he says.

'All actors have to put something of themselves into a role,' he explained in between mouthfuls of coffee. 'And I do have a kind of empathy with doctors.

Playing one is such a nice thing to do because they are a bit like magicians. People who try to ease anxiety, to alleviate pain and to whom other people look up. Whatever the time of day or night when something goes wrong it is always a case of "Get the Doctor!" And so I'm trying to play a character who is able to do these things and with a certain amount of good humour.'

I suggest to Tom that eccentric would be a more suitable adjective than humorous in his case.

'Of course I am sure there are quiet, modest surgeons,' he replies. 'But there is no point in playing a modest surgeon on television because he just wouldn't register. I think it is also true that a lot of diagnosticians think of themselves as rather superior intellectually because they have to be deductive and very sly. They have to read the signs and find other ways of making their decisions. But a surgeon can be just as in the dark, and he has no alternatives but to take a look inside the patient. If a surgeon is in any doubt he just lifts up the bonnet!'

Tom's face is wreathed in a smile. So, then, what kind of a person is Geoffrey Hoyt? Once again another of Tom's earlier remarks from the set resurfaces.

'He is a benevolent tyrant,' he says, relishing the words. 'I think it is true that people are often reassured by benevolent tyranny – after all there has been a long history of it in drama. The loving father who growls a lot – but underneath the family are certain of his affection. I have actually had letters from viewers as well as people in the medical profession who say they have been reassured by my fatherly performance. That may all seem

Gail Benson (Emma Cunningham) is not quite sure what to make of Professor Hoyt's tame goat, Esmerelda.

like a bit of a cliche, but as you will have noticed in my performance I am not averse to turning the odd cliche. Anything to produce an effect!'

He shakes with laughter: 'On television it is a matter of playing a character who is jolly and reassuring or perhaps sometimes bad-tempered but still reassuring. Always you have to try and think of ways of interesting the audience because there is such competition on television, especially between the various hospital series. Not that I watch a lot of television! What it comes down to is that we must reassure people because it would be easy – though grossly irresponsible – to subvert a hospital formula in the name of entertainment and then frighten people.'

Does he regard Hoyt as a political man?

'Yes – but not in the positive sense. He is actually very naive in the political sense. One of the things that upsets him is that he doesn't understand modern politics. He's living in the past. It hurts him when he hears the phrase, "Yesterday's Man", because he suspects he *is* one of yesterday's men.

'Indeed, it's true that anyone who doesn't understand or make an effort to comprehend the politics of their own situation is going to be an outsider. And nobody wants to be an outsider. That is certainly one of the darker areas of Hoyt's character and one which may well emerge later as a useful way of bowling me out of the series. Because they will – they'll eventually get tired of me. And I can't say I blame them because I sometimes get tired of me!'

Our conversation next turns to some of his funny experiences while working on the series. A request for such tales is food and drink to a born raconteur like Tom.

'I remember when we were working in this sectioned-off part of an NHS hospital and I got a bit bored waiting for the next shot,' he says, one hand tapping the arm of his chair. 'I was wearing my very best consultant's double-breasted pinstripe suite and decided to take a wander into one of the wards. It is incredible what a thousand-pound suit from Jermyn Street will do to patients! Just the sight of me made them feel better. There they were these real patients, taking my badge and my large voice seriously. I said to several of them, "How are you today?" and they all replied, "Oh, much better, thank you, Doctor." And then I boomed, "Well, that's how I want it to be – I want no failures here!" '

On another occasion, Tom's perambulations took him down into the basement of a hospital where he came across a group of men in a boiler room smoking cigarettes.

'They were all quite elderly, but as soon as they saw me coming they all scattered. Now elderly fellows don't really like to scatter because it can pull muscles and break hips. So I quickly shouted, "No, stop. It's all right. I'm just a charlatan!"

'The thing was that they wouldn't believe me at first, and it was only when one of them recognized me as a shagged-out old Doctor Who that they came back looking relieved. I don't smoke myself, but I didn't want to take away their pleasures. It was amazing to see the conviction the suit and badge carried – and to watch them all light up and cough their way through another ciggie!

'Funnily not long after this I met a real consultant and he looked so *amateur*. He obviously didn't spend any money on his suits. Let's hope his neurology was better than his dress sense!'

He also has an amusing story to tell from one of his episodes which contained an operation. Although Tom insists that he puts no special preparation into these scenes, he is quick to take advice from the surgical supervisor who is always on hand to make sure he does not get any specific gesture or move wrong.

'I was doing this scene in which they wanted a close-up of my hands stitching an incision. Because it was important that it looked absolutely correct, they hired this handsome young surgeon. He had to stand around for quite a time while I filmed my bit. Then they called him over to do the close-up with his hands. But as soon as the camera started rolling this chap who had probably performed the operation hundreds of times began shaking with nerves. The director had to wait quite a long time before he had calmed down enough to shoot!'

Three women have featured large in Professor Hoyt's life. Ruth Parry, the hospital's general manager; his wife, Elizabeth, whose terminal illness he had to come to terms with in the third series; and Helen Lomax, the senior consultant in the burns unit, who helped him recover from the traumas of his wife's death, and is now providing an unexpected romantic involvement in the fifth series.

'Sue Johnston is a very experienced actress and a delight to work with,' he says, 'and Dinah Stabb who plays Helen Lomax is a lovely actress and a marvellous girl. My infatuation with her is absolutely effortless to play. It is always nice when you don't have to reach for something like that in a story – even in the close-ups!'

Many viewers and several critics believe that Tom produced some of the best acting of his career during the illness of Hoyt's wife – played by Judy Parfitt – and the drama of the car crash which resulted from her death.

'It was very gratifying to know that people felt that,' he says, 'because I was playing someone who was in decline after the loss of a person very close to him. It is not easy to play that sort of thing without someone deliberately saying, "Geoffrey seems to be depressed about the loss of his wife" – which meant I had to use lots of little touches of irrationality or irritability or irascibility and it is good to know that people picked up the signals.

'Those scenes also made me appre-

Professor Hoyt (Tom Baker) required all his courage as well as his medical skills to calm down a bottle-wielding patient in the fourth series.

ciate my own wife, Sue, even more – especially her goodness and loyalty. That's where my bread is buttered – she shelters me from things, makes things possible. I don't like real life because I don't understand it and I'm no good at it. Most people want fantasy, but they keep their desire under control. I can't escape entirely, but Sue understands my anxiety. I'm never so real as when I'm entirely fictional, and never so insecure as when I have to be real, which is why I'm garrulous and try to amuse. As you may have realized, I'm fascinated by self-delusion – it's what gets us through life!'

Tom's wife, Sue Jerrard, is also in the same business, as a television director, and their relationship is the longest of his three marriages. They have now been together for fourteen years. His first marriage to Anna Wheatcroft, the daughter of the famous gardener, Geoffrey Wheatcroft, lasted for five years and produced two sons, Daniel and Piers, now both in their thirties; and he was briefly married to Lalla Ward who played his companion, Romana, in 'Doctor Who' for several years.

Tom and Sue live in a beautifully converted Victorian schoolhouse in Kent which they share with twelve Burmese cats – many of whom are named after characters from the novels of Charles Dickens, one of Tom's favourite authors. The house, which has a church and graveyard adjoining, provides an ideal environment for the cats, says Tom, who will talk just as engagingly about them as his work if given the chance. However, the very mention of the animals clearly made him anxious to be off now that he had finished filming for the week and catch the next train from Manchester back to London.

'It is very good to be in a big popular series,' he said finally to me, standing up and looking for a bin in which to deposit his empty coffee cup. 'It is fun to do and I do seem to get on well with most of the people. I believe some directors think I'm difficult, but I just get tense. The whole thing about acting is that we are spoiled. You have just witnessed a scene that was quite small but took over an hour. The actors have to stay calm. The acting may be right but the lighting is wrong. Or the actor may be off his mark or the focus puller is not happy with the picture. All of these come into it and you just have to try and stay calm and then get straight into it.

'I think it is nice to have a vast audience watching you, too. I have never had any desire as an actor other than for tumultous applause and big audiences! I cannot bear people going on about what a very worthy production I am in if no-one is watching it. I must have big audiences. In other words,' – and his eyes light up one more time before he flashes his enormous smile and disappears through the doorway as suddenly as he entered it – 'in other words, I am just an old Butlin's redcoat who has traded in his uniform for a suit and gown!'

THE DOCTOR AND THE PATIENT FROM HELL

The senior consultant in plastic surgery, Helen Lomax, played by Dinah Stabb, who was introduced in series four has quickly proved to be a determined and totally dedicated woman who is also more than a match for Geoffrey Hoyt. The two were thrown together right at the start when the temperamental surgeon, emotionally and physically scarred by his car accident, became her unwilling patient – but the passage of time has seen their relationship develop into one of the most fascinating in 'Medics'. Indeed, love is very much in the air in the fifth series . . .

Helen's domain is the new burns unit next door to the general ward on the second floor. An impressive facility, with its four-bed cubicles, well-equipped office and state-of-the-art technology for patients, it is the envy of several of her

The traumatic first encounter between Helen Lomax (Dinah Stabb) and Geoffrey Hoyt (Tom Baker). Their relationship soon took on quite a different complexion once they got to know each other.

colleagues. Indeed, their prejudices surfaced during the last series when Helen began spending some of her time doing plastic surgery on various private patients which was purely for cosmetic reasons. Yet she did not allow this to upset her equilibrium any more than when she first met Hoyt, 'the patient from hell' as the media dubbed him at the time.

'He was quite a shock to her,' the stylish and brown-haired Dinah recalls. 'This man who distances himself from everything and everyone – including the harrowing side of his job. But actually

she quickly realized that Hoyt's bombastic attempts to browbeat everyone, to roll them over, meant that it needed one hell of a woman to stand up to him. But the professional in her couldn't help applauding his skills while the academic side of her nature revelled in his intellect. The fighter in her also responded to his challenge just as the doctor in her respected his courage. So it was not long before the controlled part of her nature started to realize that Hoyt could also disturb her real feelings. Is it any wonder, then, that they should have been drawn together?'

Dinah, a woman of quiet charm who possesses a fine sense of humour, has brought an extensive career in the theatre, in films and on television into creating Helen Lomax which is, surpris-

Admiration for each other's skills has brought Professor Hoyt and Helen Lomax closer together as their friendship in 'Medics' has developed.

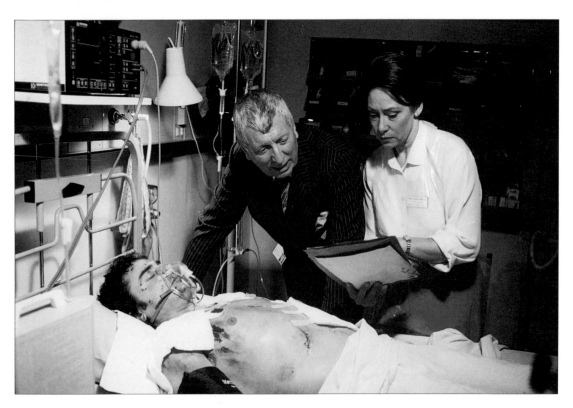

ingly, her very first medical role. No one in her family has had any connection with the hospital world, she admits, and despite playing someone who has to cope with the most horrendous burns she rather sheepisly confesses that she is 'likely to faint at a lot of things'!

Her early career saw her working at the Royal Shakespeare Company, followed by appearances at the National Theatre, the Gate Theatre, Dublin and The Crucible in Sheffield. Among her numerous film appearances have been parts in *The Riddle of the Sphinx*, *The Whistle Blower* and *The Browning Version*. On TV she has made well-reviewed appearances in every kind of production from 'Prince Regent' to 'EastEnders' for the BBC and from 'The Trespasser' to 'Prime Suspect III' on independent television.

Dinah's research for any new role is always impeccable – and 'Medics' was no exception. Before joining the series in 1994 she spent some time at the burns unit at Mount Vernon Hospital in London. Her first day was one she will never forget.

'I was very nervous,' she recalls. 'The first person I met was the young and very talented head of the burns unit who said, "Right – get scrubbed up and I'll see you in the theatre." And I thought to myself, "Do I really want to do this?" Finally, I plucked up the courage and did as he said. Then I went into the theatre and there they all were grouped around the operating table. I remember that an Ella Fitzgerald song was playing on the sound system.

'Anyhow, I walked towards the group and as I got close they just parted. And there on the table was the body of a patient and they were cutting a large fold of his skin off to overlap a huge burn. I nearly fainted on the spot. I thought to myself, "I must get out of here." So I walked out to a side room with as much dignity as I could muster and drank a glass of water. "I have to go back," I told myself, "or I'll never be able to live with myself or face any of them again." So I took a deep breath and returned to the theatre. If any of them noticed they said nothing, but I was very pleased with myself.

'Afterwards I was given a conducted tour of the ward and saw some patients with the most dreadful injuries. That night when I went home my mind was still spinning with everything I had seen and I had a terrible dream about bodies and burns. After that day everything on 'Medics' has been easy!'

Dinah's opening episode on 'Medics' provided a memorable confrontation with Geoffrey Hoyt when she mistook him for a dithering patient and he thought she was just a lowly doctor on the Henry Park staff.

'That really set the pattern of our relationship,' Dinah says. 'You could see the sparks coming off both of us and it was a wonderful acting challenge. Tom Baker is such a character and fun to work with that I've never really looked back.'

Dinah has, in fact, played the role with such conviction that in real life she has more than once been confused for a real medic.

'I was visiting a friend in Stoke Mandeville hospital and as I was walking along the ward towards her bed I was stopped by this staff nurse,' she says, a smile sparkling in her dark brown eyes. 'The staff said to me, "Haven't I seen you before?" I shook my head. "Are you sure we didn't study together?" she persisted. I could see this might go on so I put her out of her misery. "No nothing like that," I answered, "I just play a doctor on television!"'

When filming in the burns unit, Dinah looks every inch the part, however, the illusion especially augmented by the authentic props on the ward and in her office.

Photographs of the staff greet visitors, alongside a copy of the Patients' Charter, rows of get-well cards and even huge bunches of flowers. Inside Helen Lomax's neat and functional office a consulting couch dominates one corner with a light box for X-ray photographs on one side and a 'Classification and Appearance of Burns' chart on the other. The meticulous attention to detail on the part of set dressers Alan Waterfall and David Flower has even gone as far as the consultant's bookshelves which contain titles such as the *Medical Register, the*

Foetus as a Patient and *Meat Science*, while on her desk lies a neat pile of patients' brown folders – on the top of which is still one numbered 32648 inscribed with a black felt-tip pen: GEOFFREY HOYT.

Dinah Stabb is enthusiastically looking forward to her future work on 'Medics'.

'The relationship between Helen and Geoffrey Hoyt is never going to be a cosy one, you just know that,' she says. 'You can just sense that if the romance really comes to something between them then it will not be easy for either. And if they were to get married you just know they are going to be having a row the next morning. What everyone can be sure of is that nothing between this couple will be easy for even so much as one episode!'

From antagonists to lovers: Helen Lomax and Geoffrey Hoyt can see a future - of a kind - together.

THE IRON LADY FROM BROOKSIDE

IT IS PERHAPS ONLY FITTING that the office of Ruth Parry, Henry Park's 'Iron Lady', should be the only one on the top floor of Ancoats Hospital. But what invariably amuses visitors to the location is the fact that the general manager's power base where she wheels and deals to keep the hospital and its staff functioning is actually built in what was previously Cawley Ward the children's ward.

Beyond the false wooden partitions which have been erected to create the illusion of a stylishly furnished office complete with pile carpets, panelled doors and the very latest office furniture, are the poignant reminders that once small children battled for their lives in this very place. Still fixed to the walls out of the range of the television cameras are a whole series of Walt Disney posters, and piled in one corner just a few of the long-abandoned toys and games that the little patients once played with . . .

Ruth Parry's office befits a power broker in every respect. The reception area bristles with phones, computers and all the modern technological equipment of high-speed business life. Just beyond this is an alcove which contains a large circular conference table surrounded by a ring of comfortable chairs. Several bookcases along the walls are packed with medical titles; while heaps of files and computer print-outs cover a sideboard and a huge desk, all awaiting the attention of the top executive who so clearly works here. The only really personal touch is a photograph hanging near the room's one big exterior window that pictures the leading female star of 'Medics' seated with the Duchess of York, a long-time fan of the series. It is inscribed simply in ink, 'Dear Sue, With Love, Sarah, 1993.'

The Sue Johnston who appears in this picture is actually more casually dressed than the character who turns up on the screen – just as Sue herself, a slim, dark-haired lady with a warm, friendly smile is a very different person from the 'Iron Lady' of the series. Yet in the four series in which she has played Henry Park's top manager she has made the role as memorable to viewers as her earlier part as Sheila Grant in Brookside,

The 'Iron Lady' of Henry Park, Ruth Parry (Sue Johnston) with her ambitious Resources Manager Derek Foster (Nick Dunning), who has already got his eye on her job.

which she played continuously for eight years. And every bit as different.

From the put-upon wife of bullying Bobby Grant, Sue has become, in the words of one recent newspaper review, 'tough as surgical steel, sharper than a hypodermic and as unchallengeable as an NHS waiting list.'

It is a role that she relishes and talks about with frankness, interrupted by frequent bursts of delightful laughter. For there is nothing pretentious or immodest about this actress who is quick to praise her co-stars and always ready to laugh at her own mistakes. There is also, though, a very evident streak of determination in her character which was shaped by her upbringing in Warrington, Cheshire where she still lives to this day.

'Ruth is pretty ruthless and strong and it gives me great enjoyment to play her,' Sue says, smiling. 'It's lovely to be incredibly bossy and to wield all that power and handle a huge budget. But it is an enormous responsibility, too. She is a great manipulator of people – she has to be. It is a very satisfying part – but if I ever met Ruth I'm sure I would be frightened to death of her!

'I also think she is a very selfish woman. Very self-centred and very ambitious. That has been reflected in her home life which is virtually non-existent. The way it has fallen apart is very much about the way she herself *is*. It is hard to imagine that she ever had a marriage – or how she ever brought up a son.'

Sue herself was born during the Second World War and, with a career as an actress very much at the forefront of her ambitions, she trained at the Webber Douglas Academy before appearing in repertory theatre in Farnham, Salford, Lincoln, Manchester and Coventry. She became a founder-member of the M6 Theatre Company before breaking into television where she has appeared as Mrs Chadwick in 'Coronation Street'; the role which made her famous in 'Brookside' between 1982–90; and then in the memorable role of Barbara Grade who died of a muscle-wasting disease in 'Goodbye Cruel World'. Sue has been married twice – the second time to a theatre director which ended soon after the birth of her only son, Joel.

She retains nothing but fond memories of 'Brookside', and though making the decision to leave caused her considerable stress, she has since had no reason to regret her move.

'I really got to know the character of Sheila,' she recalls, 'and when you get involved in a good storyline as well it can be very exciting. In fact there was a great temptation to stay – which is a problem because actors can get caught up in something and then it's too late and you have no alternative but to stay. I think if I am honest I should have left a couple of years earlier than I did.

'In the end it was a terribly hard decision. I had been happy in 'Brookside' and, of course, I liked the security, especially with a young son to support. But I got to feel more and more restless. I was getting up, taking the same route to work, doing the job, going home – I felt I might almost be working in a bank. And because I thought I'd come to the end of the road with my character I was also worried that my career might suffer. So, in the end, I left – though with great anxiety and sadness.'

Sue's parting from the famous soap was painful in more ways than one. Her mother, she says, thought she was 'insane' to throw away the regularity the soap offered.

'In fact I got very stressed about it,' she admits. 'I worried about making a career mistake and then had the added worry of a close friend dying. I developed pains in my chest and for a time I thought I might be having a heart attack. They rushed me to hospital and I had various tests. Thankfully they declared me fit – but I reckon the pains were brought on by the sheer trauma of that period in my life.'

Sue's determination that she could not go on living her life trapped in one role has subsequently been amply rewarded.

'It is always a worry to any actor or actress that you will be typecast,' she continues. 'But since leaving "Brookside" I have done a whole range of parts and so far it seems to have worked out. I suspect that there are some people out there who still say, "Did you see Sheila Grant on the telly the other night?" – but as far as I am concerned it has all been a new lease of life . . . especially on "Medics."'

Sue was, in fact, familiar with the series when she was offered the role of Ruth Parry – for Francesca Ryan is a close friend and she had watched the opening episodes on TV. But the series was then, of course, about to become something very different.

'Apart from introducing a lot of new characters, there was also a debate about whether to change the title or not because of all the changes,' she says. 'But I was immediately attracted to the part of Ruth Parry – not least because of the fact that Granada were making the series in and around Manchester and that would enable me to live at home while I worked.'

She had, though, never played a role with any medical connections before 'Medics' – although since the success of the series she has had one slightly similar part as a receptionist in a doctors series on Radio 4. Although Sue made no conscious decision to 'trail' a real-life hospital executive in preparation for her part, she did have a role model.

'I believe that the role of Ruth is about the woman more than the job. In any event, you learn about the job as you read the scripts. I have subsequently met some chief executives and they are very bright and very powerful people – but they are also very different. So for me it was a case of working out for myself what kind of person Ruth Parry was.

'Actually I knew a woman who had reached quite a high-powered job in television through accountancy, and because this was the route that Ruth had taken to get to the top of her pile I used her as a kind of model. She was a high-flier and quite different from me. But it was still nice to have all those highly technical books in my office and sit there looking smug as if I had read them all, while in fact not being able to open one and understand anything!'

It was not long after she had started bringing the tough and self-assured Ruth Parry to the nation's TV screens that Sue, who holds strong political views and has more than once spoken out about the state of the health service, was thrown unexpectedly into a real medical drama over which she was unable to exert any control despite all the knowledge she had gleaned about the running of hospitals. Her father, Fred, who was seventy-nine, died before he could be treated for a routine cataract operation and all because of a long hospital waiting list.

'My dad loved to read and watch TV – it was about all he had left,' she says, the smile leaving her face to be replaced by the firm set of her chin which has become so familiar to viewers of 'Medics'. 'But he was deprived of even those simple pleasures. I tried to persuade him to go privately, but it was against his principles. What really distressed me was that he had already been on a waiting list for a long while. I wanted him to have it done so badly – I hated seeing him just sitting in his chair, not being able to do anything. But he never made it.'

Sue is, though, full of praise for the treatment her father received at Warrington General Hospital from Alan Massie, the young junior doctor whose death from heart problems brought the issue of the long hours worked by hospital doctors into the headlines.

'He was a really good doctor,' Sue says. 'No matter how busy he was he would always find time to sit and talk to the patients in his care. My dad was always talking about the long hours he worked. He would have been devastated to learn of Alan's death.'

Sue's own anguish was heightened by the role she was playing in 'Medics' as one of the self-same bureaucrats who are now commonplace in NHS hospitals, 'wielding balance sheets and calculators' – and she also recalls the fact that the events all occurred just before the start of the last general election campaign.

'There were all kinds of promises being made then about waiting lists,' she says ruefully, 'but just look what happened! These bureaucrats are wheeler-dealing with figures, throwing up all these percentages. Yet you and I know it is not working, so nobody is impressed by the percentage figures any more. Do you know since we began filming this series, several of the hospitals that we filmed in while they were still functioning are now closed! I am a great believer in the welfare state and it is so sad to see it crumbling.

'It is the hypocrisy of it which is most distressing. The NHS just cannot be run as a business – it is about *people*. There has to be another way. To me it is a basic right to be able to have access to treatment. Otherwise we will end up like America where people just can't get treated if they can't afford the medical insurance.'

But in her role as Ruth Parry, Sue had to swallow her private principles and get on with breathing life into her character who, she says, believes strongly in the National Health and is in favour of trusts.

'But statistics are what rule now. That is how those in charge see the world – not in terms of emotions. Ruth Parry says, "I will wheel and deal and if necessary get rid of people because it is all for the good of the hospital and therefore the good of the patient." That's the justification. But the doctors and nurses who are out there, living it, feeling it,

dealing with it on an emotional level, know that it doesn't balance that way. It's just not that simple.'

Sue attributes her political commitment to being a student in the Sixties. 'We were always up there, shouting and standing up for things,' she remembers. 'If we could only care more, things would change, but when I see everything I believe in collapsing, I almost want to run away.'

Despite these convictions, Sue Johnston has no intention of following in former actress Glenda Jackson's footsteps and become an MP. 'Definitely not. I have thought about it, because I do get quite involved, but no – I love the theatre too much.'

Ruth Parry in one of the happier moments of her job, with Geoffrey Hoyt (Tom Baker) and Tom Carey (Hugh Quarshie).

Any such decision would also no doubt be a severe blow to the makers of 'Medics' – not to mention those other producers and directors that admire her talent – who showed just how high a value they put on her contribution to the series during filming of the fourth series when they discovered her dates clashed with another engagement to which she was committed. They decided to send Ruth Parry off on a 'sabbatical' during the middle section of the series.

'I was very pleased about that,' Sue

says smiling again. 'I didn't want to lose the part becuase it is such a good one. Ruth is Mrs Assertive – everything I am not – and I love her.'

There have, in fact, been several profound changes in the life of Ruth Parry – perhaps most intriguingly the short-lived relationship with the research consultant, Tom Carey, which ended when she discovered he was 'fixing' the results of his research. Sue still grins at the memory of that period in her character's life.

'I remember when I first saw the script. I thought, "Oooh, I'm not quite sure about this!" I said to myself, "My mother will die when she sees us together." But as an actress I had to find a way to make the relationship viable – and Hugh Quarshie *was* very dishy!'

More surprises are due to follow in the fifth series.

The running of the hospital has to take second place for Ruth Parry at the start of series five when the life of her son Matthew (Oliver Milburn) is in danger. Also keeping a bedside vigil is her estranged husband Brian (Robin Ellis).

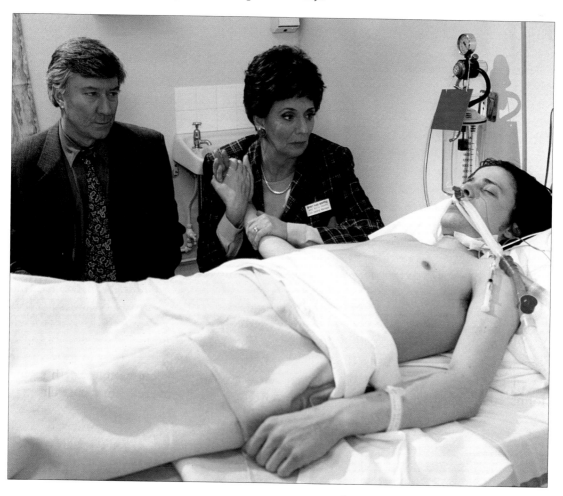

'Despite all her toughness, Ruth is starting to fall apart a little bit,' Sue admits bluntly. 'We have seen the odd bit of vulnerability in her before now. But in this next series she has to face up to her son nearly dying and an attempt at reconciliation with her husband who has been living in Europe go wrong. Plus the fact that Derek Foster, the resources manager, is at her elbow all the time looking for things to use against her to undermine her position and, if possible, get her job. There is a lot at stake for her.'

Playing Ruth's husband is Robin Ellis – famous for his role in the classic BBC series, 'Poldark'. 'It is a very interesting piece of casting,' Sue says. 'Because as the husband Robin is so soft and gentle that you just imagine him being walked all over by her – and it's no wonder their son wants to be with his father. I bet he has been more of a mother and father to him than she has ever been.

'She is also wheeler-dealing herself stupid in the hospital and making very bad mistakes. And there is the continuing local pay dispute and though she is busy manipulating as much as ever, it's not coming off as it did in the past. She's just not up to scratch – things are beginning to slip out of control for her. One of the answers she finds is in drink.'

With this tantalizing reference, Sue pauses for a moment and looks out of the window as if mentally preparing herself for the demands of the next twelve episodes of 'Medics'.

'Even her relationship with Hoyt starts coming under threat especially when she puts her foot in it very badly between him and Helen Lomax. So she falls out with both of them and feels very abandoned and extremely alone. She doesn't even have any friends to turn to because she lives all her life in the hospital. In fact, she has no life beyond it. Ruth is a very lonely lady – she has given everything to her work and is in danger of ending up with nothing.

'There is something about her – her drive – that I don't understand,' Sue adds after another pause. 'Except to say that I also love my work and I continue to work hard. But I think I have prioritized my life rather better than she has done.'

As if to demonstrate just how different she and Ruth Parry are, Sue quickly begins to talk of her son, Joel, and how well they get on. 'People keep telling me about how terrible adolescents are – but he's great. He understands my work and I've said I won't go touring until he's finished working for his exams.'

Mother and son in fact spend as much time together as possible at Sue's cottage near Warrington, and Joel for his part has occasionally been with her on political demonstrations – in particular the one they both went on in support of the miners.

Sue is also quick to produce the evidence of another of her interests, animals, with the latest batch of photographs of her new puppy, a three-month-old German shepherd dog. And when anyone offers a cigarette to this woman who is often seen on screen lighting up, Sue confesses that she doesn't smoke and what Ruth Parry is actually smoking are . . . herbal cigarettes.

Like all actors in the public eye, Sue receives her fair share of letters from fans – but so far on 'Medics' the volume has not matched the numbers she enjoyed while she was appearing in 'Brookside'.

'The thing is that Ruth Parry is not a sympathetic role, so I don't get the kind of letters I've had when I've been playing someone in trouble or suffering. That's when viewers have written to me about their own suffering or about the pain suffered by other people they know. Those that I do get on 'Medics' tend to be about my clothes! Perhaps they notice me more now – because when I played Sheila Grant nobody said anything about my clothes except how awful they were! But Ruth is really smart and I've had people asking me where I got a certain blouse from, or perhaps where I bought one of my suits.

'I think some of them write to me but don't quite know what to say, so they just end up saying, "You're a very good actress could I have your autograph?" Maybe when they see the next series and the crisis with my son or when I start drinking that will give them an angle!'

Sue loves the happy atmosphere working on 'Medics'. 'There are no huge egos around; nobody being starry or difficult. And it's great now to be in one place and not forever living out of buses!'

She particularly enjoys working with Tom Baker. 'He brightens my life,' she smiles that engaging smile again at some memory which crosses her mind from the past four years 'because he's larger than life. He makes me laugh, too. But he's a very loving and kind man. He also loves telling stories and I never tire of hearing them. I find it very easy to play scenes with him.'

In her role as the hard-bitten executive, Sue has more than once needed to put on a brave face when the unexpected has occurred during filming at a real hospital.

'I don't often get involved in the gruesome side of hospital life,' she says, 'but there was one scene where I had to watch a brain operation taking place. It was a very difficult operation and the patient actually had his head fixed into a wooden frame. I asked the neurosurgeon why this was and he explained that the frame was to keep the head absolutely still. "I really hate these operations," he added. I was a bit taken aback by this and asked him why. "Because I hate operating on people while they are *awake*." I found the whole thing really freaky.'

Sue says that she is no longer as squeamish as she used to be because of all that she has learned while working on 'Medics'.

'There was another occasion when we were filming outside this operating theatre in a working hospital,' she continues. 'Just by the doors to the theatre there was a bin and one of the members of the crew suddenly said to me, "Come and look in here." And there was this human limb lying there. The surgeons had apparently just done an amputation and the limb had been put there to be taken away and disposed of. To them it was perfectly normal!'

Her experiences have also prepared Sue for just about anything that might crop up in a storyline.

'Every time I get a script and read through it, there is bound to be something new and I can't stop myself thinking, "There's something else I could die of!" You'd be lost as an actor on "Medics" if you were a hypochondriac!'

Sue Johnston's work on the series has also given her another ambition – something else she would like to add to her already extensive list of acting achievements.

'I would actually like to play one of the doctors,' she laughs. 'I think I could handle cutting things and stitching them up. Years ago I was never able to watch programmes like "Your Life In Their Hands" – it was all that *red*! – but now I think I could do it given everything that I have learned on the set of "Medics". Can you just imagine the scene? All the doctors and surgeons in "Medics" have gone on strike and Ruth Parry is the only one there to man the fort and do the ops. Terrific fun!'

THE VILLAIN OF HENRY PARK

Derek Foster, the resources manager of Henry Park, played by Nick Dunning, is both a threat to Ruth Parry's position and 'Mr Nasty' to the rest of the hospital's medical staff. Introduced in series four, Derek has become the man to hate – an ambitious and dangerous opponent who was described on his debut as 'a cold-eyed Thatcherite administrator' by *The Times'* television critic. Indeed, with-

The 'Mr Nasty' of Henry Park Hospital, Derek Foster (Nick Dunning).

in a matter of a few episodes he had proved himself a master at manipulating the press, while behind the enigmatic smile and apparent show of concern he was revealed as a man bent on cost-cutting and ways of streamlining the management structure. And at the forefront of his ambitions was clearly securing Ruth Parry's job as the hospital's general manager.

Nick Dunning, a friendly and witty man off camera, was delighted when he discovered just how much viewers loathed Derek Foster. But what really convinced him he had got the character absolutely right was when the same verdict was delivered to him by a female friend who was also a doctor.

'My friend said she found Foster's actions morally reprehensible,' he recalls with a broad smile. 'She may have been a bit suprised when I grinned with delight at this, but I knew then that I'd got him spot-on. He's not a very nice person at all. He's manipulative and is always out to further his own ambitions.'

The interplay between Derek Foster and Ruth Parry has been there for all to see ever since the resources manager took advantage of his boss's absence on sabbatical during the fourth series to try to further his own career. The fact that he also created a massive overspend in the hospital's budget while she was away did nothing to deter his scheming.

The reason for the creation of a 'Medics' 'Mr Nasty' is explained by producer Louise Berridge.

'After series three, the character of Ruth Parry seemed to have become softened and rather mellow as a person,' she says. 'So we needed to bring in a kind of hate character, if you like. He was intended to embody the sort of political opinions that are anathema to most of the health service. I believe the outcome has been ideal: because Sue Johnston is such a sympathetic actress whereas Nick Dunning is a marvellous villain.

'We have tried not to oversimplify Foster, however, and to show that he has a human side to him as well. He is not an evil man, just as we are not saying that the policies in question are evil. What we are trying to be is pragmatic and show that there are two points of view. I think if we left that out, the series would bear no relation to reality and we would be laughed at. Everything that Foster says or does is a fair reflection of what actually happens in the medical world.'

Nick Dunning came to the series with a lot of theatrical experience behind him, not to mention having played quite a number of bad guys on film and TV. His early stage appearances included classics like *Julius Caesar* at the Chichester Festival, *Taming of the Shrew* with the RSC and *The Wandering Jew* at the National. His film roles have included *Lamb* and *London Kills Me*, while for television his talents have been successfully divided between comedy – with appearances in 'The Young Ones', 'El Cid' and 'The Rory Bremner Show' – and crime series such as 'The Bill', 'Resnick', 'Minder', 'Boon' and 'Between the Lines'. Prior to 'Medics' he also appeared in 'Casualty' and in the BBC's controversial drama, 'The Firm', about football hooliganism, in which he played a thug who appeared to be a perfectly normal professional family man – except that his life revolved around the next fight with rival soccer fans.

When he was offered the role of

Foster, Nick was spared the research of having to see the gruesome facts of hospital life at first hand.

'Foster is purely a manager,' he explains. 'He doesn't need to know how hospitals work, how doctors handle seriously ill patients or surgeons operate on heart attack sufferers or burns victims. He has to cope with finance and hospital politics and they are not so far removed from the world of business.'

He has, however, succeeded in making 'Mr Nasty' a part you love to hate with his fellow actors as well as viewers. It has become something of a tradition at every read-through of a new episode of 'Medics' that the other members of the cast hiss and boo him as he rehearses one more bit of chicanery or double dealing! (There was, however, a warm round of applause for Nick during the filming of the fourth episode of the new series when it was announced that his wife, Lise Ann had given birth to their first child, a daughter, in London.)

Although Foster's attempt to supplant Ruth Parry as general manager in the fourth series failed, his ambitions are just as keen in the fifth.

'I want the audience to be watching and waiting to see what Foster is going to do next,' says Nick. 'There is going to be a lot happening between him and Ruth Parry because they both want the number-one job. Foster is now in the humble job of resources manager and it will be interesting to see how he plots his way out of that. I know *I* want to find out!'

Louise Berridge says that Derek Foster also has another importance to the series.

'Apart from the serious issues, I think he is also funny. Humour is something there is a danger of overlooking in "Medics". Any real working hospital is full of humour – the blackest kind there is. Doctors actually laugh a lot. But we have to be careful about this element, because if we show a scene of a doctor telling sick jokes over a body then the general public would recoil in horror. They don't like to think that that sort of thing goes on. But there is no way that an intense, very solemn attitude should always prevail. It's not real – and someone like Derek Foster can be an important character to demonstrate this fact.'

THE DOCTORS IN THE HOUSE

Name: Dr Claire Armstrong
Job description: Senior Registrar
Residency: Series 1-4
Played by: Francesca Ryan

CLAIRE ARMSTRONG was the only featured doctor in the original series of 'Medics' and was the subject of the second episode, 'Claire's Story'. At thirty-four and a tutor and senior registrar at Henry Park, she was also something of a rarity in the medical ranks – one of the few women registrars specializing in neuro surgery. Noted for her cool efficiency, Claire showed herself fully aware of the changing climate for women in medicine and made herself a sympathetic figure to the four final-year medical students in her care. Her own driving ambition to obtain a consultancy position was a feature of her three subsequent series in 'Medics'.

Tall, dark-haired and strikingly attractive, Francesca Ryan known to her family and friends as Fran – was probably the first star of the series to catch the eyes and interest of viewers. It was a role, she says, that she will never forget.

'Parts like Claire's do not come up very often for an actress,' Fran recalls. 'It was a superb role to tackle because she was such a strong woman who had to face up to the dilemma that many professional women in their thirties face. Whether to pursue a career to the top of their profession or stop and have children.'

Although she was born in London – where her father was a member of the RAF – Fran as a member of a 'forces family' travelled a lot while she was a child, which has given her a wide knowledge and appreciation of the world. She decided, however, to make her home in Manchester after taking a degree at the local polytechnic. Once she had decided on acting as a career, she concentrated on the stage and quickly found herself on the move once again. A tour of Australia and Europe with the English

Opposite: Claire Armstrong (Francesca Ryan) was an unwilling recipient of Terence Harvey's attentions.

Shakespeare Company doing all the great Shakespearean plays was followed by a performance in East Berlin just before the infamous wall came down which was, she says, 'a vividly memorable event'. Like other co-star James Gaddas, Fran also has a penchant for comedy and has been for some years a member of the Comedy Express at Manchester's Contact Theatre – though she admits to finding stand-up comedy 'nerve-wracking'.

Television was still comparatively new to her when Granada offered her a role in 'Medics'.

'I had done a little work for TV,' she says. 'I was in "Brookside" for three episodes, which is where I first met Sue Johnston, who has become a dear friend. And I actually made one appearance in "Coronation Street" where I had to interview Deirdre Barlow.'

Fran's undoubted popularity playing Dr Claire Armstrong in the first series led to Granada inviting her to continue in the revamped 'Medics'. This saw her in a wider-ranging role struggling to make a go of her career as well as coping with an emotional crisis with her husband, Gavin (Ian Redford) and a love affair with her colleague Dr Robert Nevin. Claire's pregnancy and its implications for both of these men made for some of the best dramatic moments of the series.

Fran herself remembers something much more mundane about her time in 'Medics'. 'It was the clothes that Claire got to wear. She was such a smart person and always went for the top-name designer clothes. I was really spoilt, wearing the most fabulous dresses and suits.'

Her departure from the series was completely her own choice. 'I was offered a touring contract with the Royal Shakespeare Company and after all that time on television I wanted to get back to live theatre. I did agree to come back and do a few days' work on the first episode of the fourth series so that they could write out my character. And what did they do? They arranged for me to fall down the stairs in Salford Royal and crack my skull!'

Fran Ryan still retains a close interest in 'Medics' through her friendshp with Sue Johnston and the two women meet regularly. 'A lot of people have worked hard for the success of the show and it will always have the very happiest memories for me,' she adds.

Name: Dr Tom Carey

Job description: Research Consultant

Residency: Series 2-4

Played by: Hugh Quarshie

DR TOM CAREY was the man who arrived at Henry Park in a blaze of glory as the winner of the coveted research consultant in neurology post – and left under a cloud after having falsified the results of a supposed cure for Parkinson's Disease and then appropriated the research work of a colleague. The other applicant for the job whom he had beaten, Claire Armstrong, was the same person whose work on Alzheimer's Disease he had actually stolen following her tragic death.

Carey, an ambitious and charming man whose manner very nearly swept Ruth Parry off her feet during his residency at the hospital, was played with considerable panache by Hugh Quarshie, a veteran of numerous theatrical productions, films and television series.

Hugh, born in London, made his debut in *Much Ado About Nothing* at the Oxford and Cambridge Shakespeare Company, and followed this with some exciting performances in *Othello* at the Greenwich Theatre; *Whose Life Is It Anyway?* at the Savoy Theatre; plus a string of classics for the Royal Shakespeare Company and *Guys and Dolls* for the Deutsches Schauspielhaus in Hamburg. Among his film appearances have been supporting roles in *The Dogs of War, Highlander* and *Nightbreed.*

On TV his work has been equally varied from the 'Diary of Albie Sachs' to 'A Midsummer Night's Dream' and the popular legal series, 'Rumpole of the Bailey.'

Before taking on the role of Dr Tom Carey, Hugh spent some time understudying a London consultant as well as undergoing a 'crash course in medical text books so I could understand the terms I was being asked to use!'

He found the mixture of undoubted talent and unscrupulous ambition which was Dr Carey's character a fascinating challenge to put on the screen. He was also very intrigued by the fact behind the fiction of the events which he brought to the screen with such conviction.

'The story of Carey's research was actually very topical at the time,' Hugh recalls. 'He was working on a contentious line for the treatment of Parkinson's Disease. Basically it consisted of taking the brain cells from an aborted foetus while it was still alive and then injecting them into the organ in a patient's body that was failing to produce the enzyme that prevents Parkinson's. At the time we were filming, this treatment was under review by the BMA. And then a few months later they came out with a number of very strict guidelines which in effect said it was not justified. It was just too contentious – there was nothing else quite that far advanced.

'Carey also stole Claire Armstrong's research notes, of course, and presented them as his own. He was riding on this great high – presenting papers at international symposiums – but in fact it was not his work at all. So that's why he left at the end of the last series – in disgrace!'

Whether Tom Carey was in disgrace or not, Hugh Quarshie himself was quickly in demand again for television and has most recently been seen playing a good cop, Detective Chief Inspector Ron Craigh, in another of Lynda La Plante's brilliant series, 'She's Out'.

The front line of medical research: Dr Tom Carey (Hugh Quarshie) and Dr Claire Armstrong (Francesca Ryan) examining a human foetus.

Name: Dr Alison Makin

Job description: House Officer

Residency: Series 2-5

Played by: Teddie Thompson

DR ALISON MAKIN, the house officer on the chest ward, played by Teddie Thompson, was at the heart of one of the surprise storylines in the fourth series of 'Medics'. After a series of heterosexual relationships during earlier episodes – including the breakup of her marriage and quick flings with a fellow student doctor Toby Maitland-Evans (Jo Stone-Fewings) and then Dr Jay Rahman – Alison began to question her sexuality and confessed to being in love with her female boss, senior registrar Sarah Kemp (Patricia Kerrigan). The release of the news to the press that she was to fall in love with another woman immediately prompted headline stories in several of the tabloid papers, *Today* especially, which drew parallels between the series and several of the soaps: '"Medics" is following the same path as "Emmerdale", "Brookside" and "EastEnders" with a lesbian storyline shaking up the action at Henry Park Hospital.'

It was not these reports which worried Teddie Thompson, however – but what her mother and father might think about seeing her on the screen declaring her love for another woman.

'The storyline was a great challenge for me as an actress,' she recalls, 'but I couldn't help feeling sorry for my poor mum and dad. They find it hard enough watching me doing love scenes with men, let alone women. They are terribly liberal but when it comes down to it, they still look on me as their little girl. I didn't know how to tell them, but in the end I didn't have to. Charlie (Teddie's husband, BBC 2 producer Charles Pattinson) just casually dropped it into the conversation when we were all out to dinner!'

Teddie, thirty-three, is, in fact, no newcomer to the demands of acting or of playing a medical role. For it was her mother, who trained as an actress and worked as a drama teacher in her home town of Blackpool, who first made Teddie interested in acting; and while she was undergoing her training at the Bristol Old Vic Theatre she played Sister Anderson in *Whose Life Is It Anyway?* Her talent for drama was soon spotted, too, when she won the 'Theatre Student of the Year' award.

The sparkly, blonde actress honed her skills with six productions at the Salisbury Theatre – including *Chorus of Disapproval, Tess* and *Pride and Prejudice* – then *Jungle Book* with the Royal Shakespeare Company and *Pickwick* at the Northcott Theatre in Exeter. On television she has since been seen in a variety of shows including 'Inspector Morse', 'Life After Life' and in three series of 'Boon'. She made her film

debit in *I Bought A Vampire Motorcycle*.

Teddie joined the staff of 'Medics' in the revamped second series as a trainee doctor and prepared for her role by shadowing a nurse for three weeks, after which she spent several days on a ward for the terminally ill which, she says, was a profoundly affecting experience.

In fact, Teddie was called upon to shock her parents almost as soon as she was seen on the screen in the series.

'I still get a shudder when I think about it,' she says today. 'I had to cavort about half-naked in a gym for my first love scene. My dad, who is an architect, was working in Africa at the time and I didn't think for a moment that he would see it. But apparently the series was

Teddie Thompson (centre) who plays Dr Alison Makin, socializing with Dr Sarah Kemp (Patricia Kerrigan) and Dr Robert Nevin (James Gaddas).

pirated out there and he saw the episode one night. The first I knew was when I got a letter from him – but I'm not going to tell you what he said in it!'

More surprises were in store for Teddie during the fourth series when she had become house officer on the chest ward and went through a personality clash with the new senior registrar, Sarah Kemp. Alison suspected that Sarah despised her for having come up through the nursing ranks – and certainly the registrar lost no opportunity to put her down in a patronizing manner. However, in time they both learned to respect each other's different skills and with this greater understanding came friendship – which was when Alison's problems really began.

Teddie vividly remembers receiving the script which was to put her in the tabloid headlines.

'It was odd because I am completely the other way,' she says, 'I've known my husband since I was sixteen and so I've been in a steady relationship for half of my life. Anyhow, after I had re-read the script I thought it was interesting and a bit of a change for the character. This issue has been made a subject for titillation in so many different programmes, I decided I would just play it like they were just two people behaving in this way. I reckoned it shouldn't be any different than playing it opposite anyone else – it should be sensitive like any love scene. I just tried to be as normal as I could and I think the final result was educational rather than sensationalized.

'Of course, ultimately things didn't work out between Alison and Sarah – unlike the other lesbian storylines around at the time – and that made it more interesting, I believe. Alison was just confused about her sexuality and playing around with the idea. I hope that we showed that straight people can have these feelings, too.'

Working on 'Medics' has not been without its real-life dramas for Teddie. She remembers the episode when the Henry Park burns unit was put on full alert after a major fire broke out.

'What with everything else that was going on in her life, the crisis almost proved too much and Alison nearly lost her cool,' she reflects. 'she'd been through the mill emotionally and the fire acted as a kind of catalyst. Suddenly she couldn't keep her feelings bottled up any more.

'The dramatic fire sequence felt terribly real when we were filming it. I remember running along and suddenly hearing this explosion behind me. I knew it was going to happen, but I didn't realize how loud it would be – but I ended up ducking for real. My heart was *pounding*.'

Her heart was also pounding during another incident which involved her father – one in which she has cause to be grateful for all the medical information she had picked up while working on the series. The reason being that she recognized the symptoms when her father was having a heart attack and her prompt action helped to save his life.

'I had seen a heart attack "patient" in the series made up to look really grey,' she says, 'and, frankly, I didn't believe anyone could look that colour. Not long after that I went to my parents for Christmas and while Mum and I were making up my bed I noticed Dad had gone that same colour. He told me it was nothing just an ache in his arm.

'But I told Mum it was serious. It was then one o'clock in the morning, but I telephoned Dad's GP and asked him to come immediately. He agreed and said he would bring a paramedic with him. Outside it was lashing with rain and blowing a gale as it only can in the Lake District and my parent's cottage is miles from anywhere – practically in a field. So I went outside dressed up like a fisherman and kept flashing a torch, so the doctor wouldn't miss me. It seemed an age before they arrived, but they whisked

Dad into hospital and he made a good recovery.'

When not working on 'Medics', Teddie and her husband have been fully occupied repairing and refurbishing a Victorian house in a quiet conservation area of Lambeth in South London that was in an advanced state of decay when they bought it. Teddie's architect father was, of course, able to give the couple lots of advice, but they are proud of having done virtually all of the back-breaking work themselves. The result has been a dream houe restored to all its former glory thanks to their 'major surgery'.

Now, however, their tranquillity is about to be disturbed, for just prior to filming the fifth series of 'Medics', Teddie and Charlie became the second couple associated with the series this year to have a baby. Although this meant that Teddie could not return to the series for the opening episodes, she does re-appear in episode five.

'That's the magic of television,' Teddie says gratefully. 'I did want to stay with the series so they wrote me out for the first four episodes. But with the storylines getting better all the time I could hardly wait to get back. And the production staff on 'Medics' have been wonderful – they've even set up a crèche in the old nurses' quarters so that I can have the baby near me while I'm working!'

Name: Dr Sarah Kemp

Job description: Senior Registrar

Residency: Series 4-5

Played by: Patricia Kerrigan

DR SARAH KEMP, the senior registrar on the chest ward, has had to contend with the attentions of both sexes since her arrival in 'Medics' in series four. A warm and open personality, Sarah had first to recognize Alison Makin's crush on her for what it was and then found that Dr Robert Nevin wanted to push their friendship further into a relationship.

'When Sarah was introduced into the series so many of the characters seemed to be in a mess in their private lives,' says Patricia Kerrigan, whose flame-coloured hair and open, friendly face are perfect for playing a character that members of both sexes can relate to. 'It seemed the time had come for someone well-balanced to arrive on the scene. What she didn't know was how quickly her colleagues would complicate her life and how this would in turn unsettle her.'

Although Patricia Kerrigan is proud of her Scottish background, like so many of her nationality she got the wanderlust as a teenager and spent five years travelling the world, before a chance encounter in Holland finally brought her into the world of the stage and television. She grew up in Edinburgh and began her study at the tender age of sixteen with the Scottish Youth Theatre. Then, suddenly, she and a friend set off to see the world – intending only to be away for a year.

'We visited America, Australia, Singapore, Pakistan and Germany,' she recalls. 'Along the way I earned a bit of much-needed cash by picking grapes, working in a canning factory, as a barmaid and a waitress, and I even had a spell as a petrol-pump attendant. By the time I eventually got back to Britain I was twenty-two years of age and I'd lost most of my Scottish accent. When I met my mother again she thought I'd become an Australian!'

It was a sore tooth that changed the course of Patricia's life.

'We were in Germany when I decided I should return home to Scotland for some treatment to my teeth,' she says with a wide grin. 'On the way back, I decided to make a detour to visit a friend in Amsterdam who was involved with an English-speaking theatre company. While I was with her, the stage manager had to leave because his mother was unwell and so I stepped into his shoes. I ended up getting my teeth fixed there and staying in Holland for three years taking on various roles with the group. It provided me with valuable experience and gave me a head start for my eventual acting career.'

Back in the UK, Patricia has subsequently appeared in *Love's Labours Lost* and *Women Laughing* at the Royal Exchange along with *The Duchess of Malfi* and *All's Well That Ends Well* with the Royal Shakespeare Company. Prior to joining 'Medics' – her biggest role to date – she appeared in 'The Bill', 'The Adventures of Sherlock Holmes', 'Boon', 'Imaginary Friends' and 'Playing For Real'. Although now living in London, she has kept her Scottish links alive by travelling north of the border to appear in two of Scotland's most popular series – 'Taggart' and 'Dr Finlay's Casebook', the latter of which brought her into the world of medicine for the first time.

'I've never been very interested in medicine,' she confesses, 'and I'm not very good with scientific matters. So I haven't got much in common with Dr Kemp – except that we're both Scottish!'

Although Patricia spent some time researching her role, she had only once previously been in a hospital, when she was fifteen and still living in Edinburgh. 'I was dashing to the newsagent's clutching the family pool's coupon and a five-pound note,' she recalls. 'I was worried that I'd miss the deadline for submitting the coupon and I took a chance by running over a zebra crossing without looking. I was knocked down by this car and at first I was afraid I had been seriously injured because I couldn't feel my legs. But within seconds, a crowd had gathered and I was provided with a pillow and a blanket and someone called for an ambulance.

'I was well-known in the area and all the "witnesses" said that the accident was the driver's fault which was, of course, ridiculous. But what really annoyed me was that in all the confusion somebody stole the five-pound stake money before I was whisked off to hospital for a check-up. Fortunately I only had a few bruises,

The relationship between Dr Sarah Kemp (Patricia Kerrigan, standing) and Dr Alison Makin (Teddie Thompson) has been fraught with difficulties and misunderstanding from the start.

but it was the loss of the coupon that went on hurting. Suppose they had been the winning numbers!' she jokes.

Patricia has now settled comfortably into her role as the lesbian senior registrar and after the unhappy events with Dr Alison Makin is about to have a serious love affair with a new doctor, pathologist Liz Seymour (Julia Ford) in the fifth series.

Producer Louise Berridge explains this latest twist in the story of 'Medics': 'Liz was initially intended to be a love interest for Sarah, but I am anxious to make sure that isn't all she becomes. I see her as a way of dealing with Sarah's real problem which is her inability to admit to anybody that she is gay. She hides it from her colleagues. I would like her life to move on as a result of her relationship with Liz so that she can actually walk into the Henry Park canteen and say, "So, I'm gay so what?" and then start getting on with living. Because the way things are at the moment we have this great doctor who is so straightforward in everything – but, astonishingly, there is this one bit of her life which is so screwed up. She just has to work on it.'

The challenge is one that Patricia Kerrigan relishes and one for which her ancestry has undoubtedly prepared her well. 'I believe having Scots roots is important – it's a matter of temperament. You see the Scots tend to put their cards on the table, whereas the English are more secretive . . .'

Name: Dr Diana Hardy

Job description: Consultant

Residency: Series 5

Played by: Gabrielle Drake

DR DIANA HARDY is a consultant at North Ridge Hospital, played by Gabrielle Drake, who works with Jay Rahman in the new series. A doctor of great skill, she is probably the leading researcher in the field of Gastroenterology and a woman whose beauty also hides a singleminded and at times ruthless ambition. Apart from breaking some of the unwritten rules of research during the course of her work, Dr Hardy is also not above breaking male hearts.

Gabrielle Drake has played a beautiful heartbreaker many times before in her wide and varied career on the stage and in films and television. Indeed, the vivacious red-head with melting green eyes is already being described as the most beguiling villain to be seen in 'Medics'.

'Although no one suspects the fact when Dr Hardy first appears at Henry Park,' Gabrielle explains, 'she is quite capable of using young doctors to further her own career and has no scruples about employing her femininity to blind them to what she is really up to. She is very singleminded about her job and has no intention of letting anyone put anything over her – especially not a man.'

Gabrielle has been a popular figure on British television since the Seventies when she came to fame as Jill Hammond in the long-running BBC series, 'The Brothers', about a family in the haulage business dominated by their widowed mother. Starring Jean Anderson, Richard Easton and Robin Chadwick the serial was for several years considered 'essential' Sunday-night viewing and made stars of Kate O'Mara and Gabrielle Drake.

Born in Lahore, Pakistan, Gabrielle actually worked as an au pair in Paris before following her childhood ambition to become an actress and enrolling at RADA in London. After two years of training she began treading the boards in London and her early stage appearances included *Tea Party, Noises Off* and *Court in the Act*. In the movies she has co-starred in *There's a Girl in My Soup* and an appropriate piece of casting in *Au Pair Girls*. Gabrielle followed her success in 'The Brothers' with a whole range of television work from costume dramas such as 'The Importance of Being Earnest' and 'Wellington', to a stint as Nicola Freeman in the popular soap, 'Crossroads'.

In the fifth series of 'Medics', Diana Hardy's main interaction will be with Jay Rahman who is also passionately interested in the same line of research she is pursuing. Producer Louise Berridge explains the development of their relationship.

'Diana is the number one in the

field gastroenterology and as this is Jay's passion, too, it seems natural for them to work together,' she says. 'In fact, this is the ultimate for Jay: he is proud to be in the same room as her, to read the notes she has written. But she is also an incredibly attractive woman and, naturally, he soons starts to fancy her. This is despite his on-going relationship with Gail which, not surprisingly, soon starts to go through a rough patch.

'But this relationship between Jay and Diana is not quite as simple as it may seem at first. For she is soon using him and, though it is not obvious at first, she is really a villain. Or perhaps I should say a villain in a sense we might consider totally unreasonable – although the medical world is full of them. For anyone who has reached a position of emi-nance such as Diana's has almost certainly used young doctors, got the research work out of them, and then said "Goodbye!" and published the results as his or her own. It is a very distressing thing to say, but absolutely true.

'It is this very singlemindedness – "I need to find out"; "I have got to push back the frontiers" – which enables Diana to squash people and it is this directness in her that Jay admires although he becomes one of her victims. She is really going to test him and his principles.'

The seductive Dr Diana Hardy (Gabrielle Drake) with her latest admirer Dr Jay Rahman (Jimmi Harkishin).

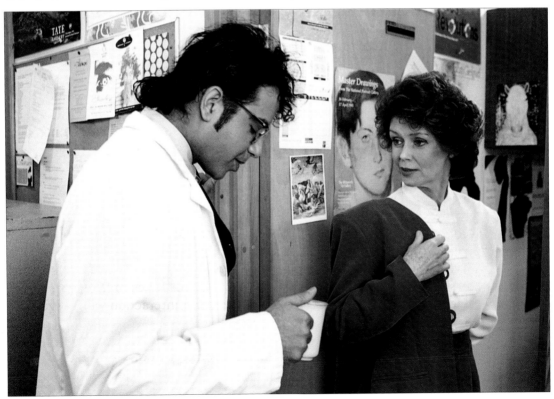

Name: Peter Vance

Job description: General Surgeon

Residency: Series 5

Played by: Ian Shaw

PETER VANCE is the second major character to be introduced in the fifth series of 'Medics'. Played by Ian Shaw, he is a surgeon from a different background and with a quite different attitude to his work to Henry Park's current top incumbent, Geoffrey Hoyt. Indeed, his very presence in the operating theatre will make sparks fly between the two men.

Ian, the son of actor Robert Shaw, is no stranger to medical drama, having appeared not long ago in 'Casualty'. Viewers have also seen him recently in two other very successful TV series, 'Soldier, Soldier', playing Gibson, and co-starring as Lieutenant Ayres with Sean Bean in 'Sharpe's Gold'.

Born in London, Ian obtained a BA honours degree in American Studies at Sussex University before changing the course of his life and signing on as a post-graduate student at the Webber Douglas Academy of Dramatic Art. His leading stage roles have been as Mercutio in *Romeo and Juliet*, Richard in *The Lover* and Malvolio in *Twelfth Night*. Ian has also appeared in the movie *Moondance*, and his other television work has included two major BBC productions, 'Century', directed by Stephen Poliakoff, and in the role of Captain Alex McLean in 'Blood and Water' an episode of 'Ghost Hour'.

Apart from trailing a surgeon for his research, Ian also brings a wide range of social skills to his part including singing, horse riding, scuba diving and considerable expertise as a rapier and foil fencer. As Peter Vance, however, he will combine a blunt wit with a sureness of touch in the operating theatre.

Louise Berridge explains the future of this intriguing surgeon in his thirties who can also be absolutely charming.

'He is a young general surgeon who will provide a link between the surgery department and the other doctors,' she explains. 'At the moment it is difficult for people like Geoffrey Hoyt and Helen Lomax to communicate with the others without stretching credibility because they are surgeons and the rest are physicians. But he is also going to present a threat to Hoyt because he represents a whole new generation of surgeons.'

Vance, in fact, comes from a completely different background to the consultant surgeon. He is a grammar school boy – the first member of his family to become a doctor – and apart from being brilliant at his job is also without the political survival instinct that characterizes the older generation of surgeons.

'He just doesn't understand that you should grovel to consultants which means that he easily rubs people up the wrong way,' Louise continues. 'He just sees one thing – "There is a patient and I want to make him better – that's what he came into medicine for." He's not going to let ethics crash in all over the place.'

Vance has been trained in all the latest surgery techniques including keyhole surgery – which means he has a far wider ranging expertise than Hoyt. An operation that may take the older man all day to perform, he can do in a fraction of the time.

'He is really going to unsettle Hoyt,' Louise adds. 'It is something we love to do. In the past series Geoffrey has been taken on by people of his own seniority – consultants such as Reginald Girling (Anthony Bate) in series three and Professor Douglas Beaumont (Ronald Pickup) in series four – but this time he is faced by a rising young star. A man who already has certain degrees of eccentricity in his character and you can sense that he will be Hoyt in thirty years time. He will drop into the pond of Henry Park like a stone!'

Louise says that apart from his skills, Peter Vance also has a will to win through despite all the odds. He is very much a gambler.

'If you are not a gambler you shouldn't be in surgery,' she concludes. 'When a body is open on the operating table no surgeon can say, "Oh, I don't know." You just have to work out what to do. And Peter Vance has that. If anything, he has it to an excessive degree. The question is going to be with all these factors at work – will he survive?'

Ian Shaw as the thrusting new surgeon Peter Vance, whose arrival at Henry Park presents Geoffrey Hoyt with a challenge on the medical front.

PRODUCTION TEAM

Executive Producer . . . . .Sally Head

Producer . . . . .Louise Berridge

Assistant Producer . . . . . .Elizabeth Bradley

Script Associate . . . . .Gwenda Bagshaw

Production Supervisor . . . . .Bill Leather

Production Manager . . . . .Terry Reeve

Production Designer . . . . .Paul Rowan

Art Director . . . . .Chris Stephenson

Continuity . . . . .Dorothy Friend

First Assistant Directors . . . . . . .Ian Galley

. . . . .John Friend Newman

Second Assistant Director . .Claire McCourt

Production Co-ordinator . . .Lynnette Carroll

Production Secretary . . . .Cathy McLoughlin

Casting Director . . . . .Judi Hayfield

Casting Assistant . . . . .June West

Script Editors . . . . .Bronagh Taggart

. . . . .Philip Shelley

Director of Photography . . . .Lawrence Jones

Camera Operator . . . . . .Gordon McGregor

Focus Puller . . . . .Alan Fraser

Clapper Loader . . . . .Steve Woods

Third Assistant . . . . .Craig Vance

Sound Recordist . . . . .Chris Atkinson

Boom Operator . . . . .Gary Kan

Film Editor . . . . .Dave Cresswell

Dubbing Editor . . . . .Paul Dickerson

Prop Buyer . . . . .Dave Livesey

Costume Designer . . . . .Sue Peck

Costume Supervisor . . . . . . .Kay McIntosh

Dressers . . . . .Roy Charters/Jackie Law

Make Up Supervisor . . . . .Margaret O'Keefe

Make Up Assistant . . . . .Claire Heron

Grips . . . . .Bob Gregory

Assistant Grips . . . . .Steve Gregory

Lighting Gaffer . . . . .Peter Hudson

Chargehand ASM . . . . .Peter Norrey

Action Props . . . . .Tony Marks

Prop Dressers . .Alan Waterfall/David Flower

Graphics . . . . .Phil Buckley

Producer's Secretary . . . . . . .Sarah Reynolds

Production Finance . . . . .Lynne Briant

MEDICS DAILY CALL SHEET

MEDICS - P1664/29030   NO:12
DAILY CALL SHEET

DATE: MONDAY 10th APRIL
CREW CALL: 0800-1900
MU/COS: 0700-1930

CONTACT:
Production Office: Lynnette Carroll
Production Manager: Terry Reeves
2nd Assistant: Claire McCourt

LOCATIONS:
NO DRINKING, EATING, **SMOKING** ON SET PLEASE.

ANCOATS HOSPITAL, OLD MILL STREET, ANCOATS, M4
GROUND FLOOR, CANTEEN.

SCENES IN SHOOTING ORDER: ****AMENDED ORDER FROM SCHEDULE:****

EP/SC	PAGE	SET	S/D	TIME	CHARACTERS
3/56	141-142	INT DOCTOR'S MESS	NIGHT 1	2215	GAIL, JAY, BILLY, LIZ, SARAH, FOSTER, JANICE, PENNY, ROBERT
3/49 PART	126	INT CORRIDOR OUTSIDE DRS MESS	NIGHT 1	2000	RUTH, BILLY, JANICE, SARAH, LIZ, JAY, GAIL, FOSTER
4/54	105-106	INT CORRIDOR NR LIFTS	DAY 3	0820	ROBERT, GAIL
3/49 PART	126	INT CORRIDOR OUTSIDE DOCTORS MESS	NIGHT 1	2000	RUTH
4/3	3-4	INT CANTEEN	DAY 1	0820	HOYT, HELEN, LIZ, SARAH, BILLY, FOSTER
3/18	43-45	STAIRCASE	DAY 1	1045	COTTERELL, FOSTER
4/76	135	INT GEN MED WARD	NIGHT 3	1808	HASTINGS, TOM, HOYT
4/42	80-81	INT GEN MED WARD	NIGHT 2	1900	JANICE, HASTINGS, GAIL
4/46	89-90	INT GEN MED WARD	NIGHT 2	2000	TOM, HOYT, HASTINGS

ARTISTE:	CHARACTER:	P.UP:	M.UP:	COS:	ON SET:
EMMA CUNNINGHAM	GAIL BENSON	0700	0715	0745	0845
PATRICIA KERRIGAN	SARAH KEMP	0730	0745	0800	0845
JULIA FORD	LIZ SEYMOUR	0730	0800	0745	0900
ROSIE CAVALIERO	PENNY MILNER	O/T	0715	0800	0845
SUSAN MCARDLE	JANICE THORNTON	0715	S/BY	0730	0930
SUE JOHNSTON	RUTH PARRY	O/T	0845	0945	1000
JIMMI HARKISHIN	JAY RAHMAN	0745	0800	0815	0845
NICK DUNNING	DEREK FOSTER	0845	0900	0915	0930
JAMES GADDAS	ROBERT NEVIN	0730	0815	0800	0845
CLARENCE SMITH	BILLY CHESHIRE	O/T	0830	0800	0900
DINAH STABB	HELEN LOMAX	O/T	1000	1100	1130
TOM BAKER	PROFESSOR HOYT	1045	1115	1100	1130
DAVID LYON	CLIVE COTTERELL	1215	1230	1245	1400
GERARD ROONEY	TOM DONNELLAN	1132	1245	1230	1530
RONALD HINES	IAN HASTINGS	1445	1500	1515	1530

SUPPORTING ARTISTES:

0715	AT GTV:	1 x PORTER, 1 x PATIENT IN WHEELCHAIR
		2 x NURSES, 1 x VISITORS
		2 x NEW VISITORS, 4 PATIENTS
		1 x AUXILIARY, 1 x NURSE, 1 x STAFF,
		1 x NEW PORTER
		2 x CANTEEN STAFF
		16 x PARTY GUESTS RE-CALLED

TOTAL = 33

ACTION VEHICLES: NONE

SPECIAL REQUIREMENTS: PARTY SCENES – ¼" PLAYBACK, MUSIC, SMOKE MACHINE.

CATERING:

0745	Breakfast to be available - 37 CREW, 10 ARTISTES, 33 EXTRAS
1300	Lunch - 37 CREW, 7 ARTISTES, 17 EXTRAS
PM:	Break

TRANSPORT:

0700	MINIBUS:	COST/M/UP/ADs	GTV-LOC
0700	CAR:	EMMA CUNNINGHAM	CLAIRE'S-LOC
0715	MINIBUS X 2:	EXTRAS X 33 SUSAN MCARDLE	GTV-LOC
0730	CAR:	JAMES GADDAS, PATRICIA KERRIGAN,	
		JULIA FORD	HOME, V&A-LOC
	O/T	ROSIE CAVALIERO	HOME-LOC
	O/T	DINAH STABB	HOME-LOC
0745	MINIBUS:	JIMMI HARKISHIN	HOME-LOC
	O/T	CLARENCE SMITH	HOME-LOC
0845	CAR:	NICK DUNNING	V&A-LOC
1045	CAR:	TOM BAKER	C'FIELD-LOC
1132	MINIBUS:	GERARD ROONEY	PICC STN-LOC
1215	CAR	DAVID LYON	V&A-LOC
1445	CAR:	RONALD HINES	V&A-LOC

ADVANCED SCHEDULE:	**TUESDAY 11TH APRIL:**
	CORRIDOR OUTSIDE HOYT'S OFFICE/OPERATING
	THEATRE/LECTURE THEATRE/HENRY PARK CORRIDOR
	ANCOATS: 2ND FLOOR LANDING/OPERATING THEATRE
	SUITE/1ST FLOOR/1ST FLOOR CORRIDOR OUTSIDE
	CHEST WARD

CREW:	0800-2000
COS/M/UP:	0700-2030

4/40, 4/41, 3/24, 3/19, 4/17, 4/48, 4/50, 4/78

NOTES:

1. 1700 APPROX JULES BURNS, MANAGING DIRECTOR, WILL BE VISITING THE SET.
2. SALLY COUSINS, PRESS OFFICER LONGON, WILL BE ON SET.
3. PETER BULLOCK, MATURE STUDENT, WILL BE ON SET.

NB. ALL PARTS OF ANCOATS HOSPITAL ARE FULLY PROTECTED BY HEAT **AND** SMOKE DETECTORS. BE VERY CAREFUL IN POSITIONING LAMPS.

ALL VISITORS/GUESTS TO THE SET MUST BE AUTHORISED BY TERRY REEVE (PRODUCTION MANAGER) AND MAKE YOURSELF KNOWN, ON THE DAY, TO THE FIRST OR SECOND ASSISTANT.

JOHN FRIEND NEWMAN - FIRST ASSISTANT DIRECTOR